an A to Z of Places and Things Saudi

An A to Z of Places and Things Saudi

published by
Stacey International
128 Kensington Church Street
London W8 4BH
Tel: 020 7221 7166 Fax: 020 7792 9288

ISBN: 1 900988 402

CIP Data: A catalogue record for this book is available from the British Library.

Design: Sam Crooks & Kitty Carruthers
Printing & Binding: Oriental Press Dubai

PHOTO CREDITS:
P7 King Faisal Foundation; pp11, 172 Lisa Greenberg; pp20, 212 ffotograff; p24 Thierry Mauger; p28 Gunnar Bemert; p 51 Alan Dickson; pp69, 158, 204 Ionis Thompson; p118 ERDWA; 127 Ruth Hawley; 154 Martyn Best; p177 Andrew Thompson; 217 Alan Pomering. All other pictures Stacey International.

an A to Z of Places and Things Saudi

Kathy Cuddihy

A note on transliteration

To make this book more readable for the layman, Arabic words have been transliterated in the form likely to be most familiar to English speakers (e.g. *hejira, suq*). With the same aim, plurals are given by the addition of an 's' to the transliterated word, rather than the transliteration of the Arabic plural. With very few exceptions, diacritical marks have been sacrificed in favour of ease of reading.

For Ayla

A

ABAYA. From neck to ankle, Saudi women shroud themselves in public in a black outer garment called an *abaya*. Islam stipulates that women should dress modestly and hide their shape from anyone who is not a member of the family. In the Gulf region, *abayas* evolved as the response to this religious requirement,

Abayas are made of silk or synthetic fabrics. Originally, the garment was kept closed by raising each side of the fabric in turn and securing it under the opposite arm. In recent years, Westerners have been obliged to wear the *abaya*. Because they are less adept at keeping the front closed while using their arms, many styles now include fastenings which allow more freedom of movement. There is also a trend towards making this otherwise drab covering into a fashion statement, incorporating designer diamantés, silver threads or beautifully embroidered borders. No matter how simple or elaborate the *abaya,* as far as full concealment is concerned, there can be no compromise. *See also* BURQA; TARHA; WOMEN'S DRESS.

ABHA. Abha's high altitude has always made it a popular summer retreat. Now, with the easing of restrictions on tourism, this capital of the rugged southwestern province of

Asir has become one of the Kingdom's main tourist destinations.

Abha serves as a convenient base for exploring Asir's many natural beauty spots, although the city itself offers little in the way of interesting sights. The Shada Palace, built in 1927 and a former office/residence for Asir governors, is now a museum exhibiting regional handicrafts and examples of Asir's traditional lifestyle. The Tuesday market is also worth a visit. Visitors particularly like to buy the locally-made, brightly-coloured baskets. *See also* ASIR; ASIR NATIONAL PARK.

ADOPTION. In Saudi Arabia, accepting responsibility for an orphaned or abandoned child is governed by the rules of Islam. If, for whatever reason, it becomes necessary to place a child with others, they should be as closely related as possible. In the case of foundlings, the child is cared for 'in trust' and becomes a 'client' of the new parents, a 'brother/sister in faith'.

In order to qualify to adopt in Saudi Arabia, the prospective parents are carefully vetted by a social worker to ensure that they are Muslims of good standing. After adoption, social workers make spot checks of the home to make sure that conditions continue to meet the necessary standards. School grades, particularly those pertaining to religious education, are also reviewed. The Saudi government provides a child support allowance up to the age of 18.

AGRICULTURE. Saudi Arabia's vast expanses of desert and scarcity of water have always been an impediment to the development of agriculture. For the most part, farming was concentrated in oases, such as lush Al-Ahsa in the east and the southwest Asir and Tihama regions, where rainfall and groundwater are sufficient to sustain regular growth.

Although the yields were modest, any surplus was used as a valuable trade commodity. Only a few areas could produce food in commercial quantities.

Traditional agriculture involved ingenious methods of irrigation and, in the mountainous regions, terracing. The main crops were coffee, dates, grains, and such vegetables as onions and tomatoes.

Sedentary farmers relied on nomadic bedouin to graze and breed their livestock, particularly camels, as they travelled to the best pastures. This service was provided in exchange for food and other provisions. Because improved methods of irrigation and modern technology have led to an increase in arable land, and because more bedouin are joining settled communities, pastoral nomadism is rapidly declining.

The substantial oil revenues of the boom years of the 1970s and 1980s brought affluence and wider opportunities to the Saudi population, causing many to abandon the hardships of farming. The government was able to revive the industry only by major investment in the infrastructure (including irrigation systems and transportation networks), the distribution of land, and generous financial incentives and assistance. As a result, Saudi Arabia became self-sufficient in the production of a number of foodstuffs and an important exporter of wheat and dates. Between 1975 and 1995, cultivated land increased from 370,000 acres to more than 14 million. Agriculture is now second only to the petroleum industry in importance.

Today, the farming industry employs nearly 48 per cent of the population. This includes nomadic herders, subsistence farmers, and the huge commercial farms. Unlikely as it seems, this land, composed mostly of deserts, has the largest integrated dairies in the world.

Concerns about adequate water supplies continue. The

government encourages farmers to diversify away from water-intensive crops and to improve methods of irrigation. This has led to an increase in the growth of crops such as fruit, vegetables, alfalfa, and rice. The improved yield has in turn resulted in a serious depletion of non-renewable aquifers and a need to import massive quantities of fertilizer, equipment, and manpower. Production levels can only be maintained through continued government subsidies. *See also* DAIRIES; DATES.

AL-AHSA (AL-HASA). The fertile oasis between Riyadh and the Gulf coast is the most extensive in the Kingdom and one of the largest in the world. The root of the region's name means 'an abundance of spring and underground water'. Al-Ahsa's impressive irrigation and drainage system is one of the largest in the Middle East.

The region of Al-Ahsa forms a part of Saudi Arabia's Eastern Province and is bounded by the Arabian Gulf on the east and Oman, UAE and Qatar on the south. It comprises four cities (Hofuf, Al-Mubarraz, Al-Oyun and Al-Umran) and as many as 60 scattered villages. The main city, Hofuf, is considered to be the date capital of the world.

Although there is evidence that the lush oasis has been inhabited for more than 6,000 years, during its more recent history control of the area passed back and forth between the Ottoman Empire (1549-1680 and 1871-1913), who referred to the region as Lahsa, and the Bani Khaled tribe, ancestors of the Al-Saud ruling family. King Abdul Aziz Al-Saud, the first monarch of the modern Saudi state, seized control of Al-Ahsa in 1913. Jurisdiction of the area has remained unchallenged ever since.

Today, Al-Ahsa offers the visitor the opportunity to explore numerous historical sites and places of interest:

ancient forts and castles, hot springs, and caves. Seventeen kilometres from Hofuf is the site of the Juwatha Mosque, where the Prophet Muhammed is said to have led the Friday prayer. *See also* HOFUF.

AL-BAHA. With an area of only 10,690 square kilometres, Al-Baha is Saudi Arabia's smallest province. It is located in the southwest of the Kingdom, between the better-known cities of Taif and Abha. The province's more than 900 tiny villages comprise picturesque communities where the people contentedly herd their flocks, tend their fields, and raise their families as their ancestors before them have done.

No industry pollutes Al-Baha's refreshing climate. During the long summer days, fresh mountain breezes offer welcome respite from the hotter lowland temperatures. In winter, the mountain population can escape the chill by descending to Al-Baha's warm coastal plains. Rains fall most heavily during spring and autumn but sporadic showers can occur any time. After a good downpour, wildflowers miraculously overwhelm the hillsides and olive and juniper forests flaunt a new density of foliage.

Modern roads connect small villages and link the province with the rest of the Kingdom. The most impressive of these roads is a 45-kilometre highway which snakes over formidable terrain in a seemingly vertical descent from 2,500 metres to sea level. The construction of 34 tunnels and 67 bridges was needed to overcome the many major physical obstructions.

Al-Baha's recorded history began some 2,000 years ago. In approximately 115 BC in the Kingdom of Sheba, or Saba as it was called (now Yemen), the great Ma'arib Dam collapsed. Deprived of this plentiful and vital supply of water, the people were forced to migrate to other parts of the peninsula. The Al-Azd tribe chose to settle in Al-Baha because of its climate, safety, and lush vegetation. From the Al-Azd are descended the region's two main tribes: Ghamid and Zahran. This familial bond has served them well over the centuries. Ghamid and Zahran have always remained strong allies – an exceptional achievement considering the rivalry and wars so common to other tribes.

Al-Baha's beauty and tranquility are clearly conducive to creativity, for some of the progeny of these tribes have made indelible marks on Arab literature and history. The renowned 6th century poet Al-Khalil ibn Ahmed Al-Farahidi is credited with establishing the standards for style and rhythm in Arabic verse. The region continues to spawn a generous proportion of the country's finest poets.

Almost 200 years after the death Al-Khalil, another landmark literary figure, Muhammed ibn Al-Hassan bin Durayd, earned repute for his learned writings on the Arabic language. By this time Al-Baha had a history of settled and sophisticated communities.

Islam, too, had its heroes from Al-Baha. In the time of the Prophet Muhammad, the Zahran tribe sent a delegation headed by Al-Tufail ibn Amr Al-Dousi to Makkah to listen to the Prophet and decide whether the tribe should heed his words. The elders of the powerful Quraish family received Al-Tufail in Makkah and tried to discourage him from having any contact with the Prophet. Al-Tufail refused to give in to the pressure. Impressed with the message of the *Qur'an*, he adopted Islam and returned to Zahran (Al-Baha) to convert others.

The region encompasses a number of historically important places, including the rediscovered town of Asham which once enjoyed great prominence as a gold mining centre. Archaeologists suggest that the civilization at Asham must have achieved a high level of culture. Writings discovered so far reveal several exquisite styles of Arabic script. Even the gravestones are exceptional, giving comprehensive descriptions of the persons buried.

AL-DAHNA DUNES. Al-Dahna is a 644-kilometre long sandy arc that is up to 48 kilometres wide. It links the Nafud desert in the north with the Empty Quarter in the south. The red colouring of the dunes results from a coating of iron oxide on the grains of sand. *See also* DESERT; EMPTY QUARTER; NAFUD.

AL-FAISALIAH. A spectacular sound-and-light show in May 2000 marked the inauguration of Riyadh's luxurious Al-Faisaliah Centre. Its distinctive 267-metre tower makes it the Kingdom's first skyscraper.

Designed by the renowned British architect Lord Foster of Thameside, the US$320 million multi-use project is built on a 55,000 square metre site that comprises the landmark tower, the 5-star Al-Faisaliah Hotel, luxury apartments, shopping mall, and a banquet and conference hall which is the largest non-military column-free space in Saudi Arabia. Each component of Al-Faisaliah encourages cross-trading opportunities and reflects gilt-edged luxury and state-of-the-art technology.

The prestigious complex is owned by the King Faisal Foundation, the Middle East's foremost philanthropic

The fireworks during the opening celebration of Al-Faisaliah tower light up the night sky.

organization. All profits generated from Al-Faisaliah will help to support the Foundation's many projects worldwide.

AL-FAU. Although this site boasts no architectural masterpieces like Madain Saleh, the treasures unearthed at Al-Fau are probably the most important pre-Islamic finds so far discovered in the Kingdom.

Saudi Arabia's Department of Antiquities began excavations in 1972. The site covers more than two kilometres from north to south and approximately one kilometre from east to west. Located on the famous frankincense route on the edge of the formidable Empty Quarter, Al-Fau saw the peak of its prosperity roughly between the years 200 BC and AD 400. Numerous water wells and cisterns, paintings of hunting scenes, animal bones, and evidence of agriculture indicate that a formerly moderate climate allowed flora and fauna to flourish.

So far, archaeologists have excavated the remains of what appears to have been a flourishing market town. A large *suq* area supports the theory of Al-Fau's importance as a trading centre. The discovery of fine linens and beautiful frescoes as well as many other precious and sophisticated items indicate a refined and wealthy culture.

King Saud University, Riyadh, has a small but captivating exhibition of some of the intricately crafted gold jewellery, household items, and other artefacts from the site.

AL-JAWF. This northwestern province of Saudi Arabia abuts the borders of Jordan and Iraq. A ring of sandstone mountains surrounds flat lowland plains that drift into the great Nafud desert. Evidence of ancient inland seas exist at Al-Juba and Wadi Sirhan. The lava plateau at Al-Harrah, home of an important wildlife conservation area, is another interesting geological feature of the province.

The largest concentration of Al-Jawf's population of 200,000 lives in Sakaka, the capital. Other principal towns are the historically important Dumat Al-Jandal, Tarbayil, a farming district, and Garayat, the town bordering Jordan.

Fertile land and deep artesian wells have made agriculture the region's main source of income. Al-Jawf's reputation for fine olives has been acclaimed for thousands of years. Dates are also an important crop.

The tradition of weaving, abandoned in most other parts of the Kingdom, survives and thrives in Al-Jawf. Women continue to spin, dye, and weave the thick wool of the local goats, sheep, and camels into distinctive carpets and decorative tapestries, bags, and other accessories. A renewed appreciation for this craft has made some of the finer pieces much sought after for their quality and artistic interpretation.

Thanks to the fact that Al-Jawf is included on Saudi Arabia's newly burgeoning tourist trail, the rich archaeological heritage is being rediscovered. The influence of Babylonians, Nabataeans, Romans, and Byzantines have all left their marks on the region. This summer camping destination for nomads was the political and commercial centre for early Arabian tribes and the crossroads of the major trade routes to Palestine, Syria, Iraq, Tabuk, and central Arabia. Its coordinates are no doubt what inspired the post-Islamic name Al-Jawf, meaning 'strategic position'.

The oasis town of Dumat Al-Jandal,

The minaret of the Umar bin al-Khattab Mosque in Dumat Al-Jandal.

A

referred to as Dumah in the Bible, was the site of the earliest recorded settlements. Eventually the community became strong enough to declare itself an independent state, the first on the Arabian peninsula. The ancient walled fortress Qasr Marid still stands sentinel over the town. Construction of the massive stone and mud brick structure is attributed to a grandson of Abraham.

Near the fort is the Omar ibn Al-Khattab Mosque, named after the second caliph. It is one of the earliest surviving mosques. The minaret probably predates its subsequent religious function since its orientation differs slightly from the rest of the building. Its construction techniques more closely resemble those of the adjacent well-preserved village which dates from the time of the Prophet. Dumat Al-Jandal's town wall, which is undergoing excavation, is believed to have been built by the Nabataeans.

Just outside Sakaka, sites of special interest include the Qasr Zabal, a hilltop castle believed to be pre-Islamic, and Bi'r Saisara, a Nabataean well leading to underground irrigation channels. Al-Rajajil is a deserted plain with approximately 50 groups of unexplained standing stones believed to date from 4000-2000 BC. The tall, slim flint stones (the tallest is 3.5 metres x 75 centimetres wide) have Thamudic graffiti and are oriented in the sunrise/sunset sight lines. It is believed this was the site of an ancient cult. Pottery shards, mysterious inscriptions, and rich displays of petroglyphs all contribute to the archaeological fascination of the region. *See also* DESERT; NAFUD.

AL-KHOBAR. Al-Khobar first sprang up in 1923 as a tiny village on the Arabian Gulf coast in what is now Saudi Arabia's Eastern Province. Fishing and pearling provided the embryonic community with its livelihood.

The construction of the huge Aramco camp in the 1930s brought prosperity and rapid growth to the village. In addition to increased trade opportunities from the sudden influx of petroleum personnel, Al-Khobar's importance grew as crude oil was shipped from its pier to Bahrain for processing. Al-Khobar has continued links with Bahrain, serving as a gateway to the island: it is the point of entry to Saudi Arabia from Bahrain via the King Fahd Causeway. Al-Khobar is the smallest city in the Dhahran-Al-Khobar-Dammam triangle that is the heart of the Kingdom's oil industry. *See also* EASTERN PROVINCE; KING FAHD CAUSEWAY.

ARAB BREAD. The ubiquitous wheat-based flat bread, called *khubz arabi* in Arabic and referred to as pita, Arab, or pocket bread in English, is a staple of the Saudi diet. It is served as a bed and accompaniment for rice, meat, and vegetable dishes and as a handy scoop for foods such as *hommos, tabouleh*, and *baba ghanouj*. *Manaeesh*, Arab bread that has been garnished with a light coat of oil and sprinkled liberally with *zatar* before baking, is popular at breakfast. People in the Hijaz love *tamees*, a stamped flat bread topped with sesame seeds and served with white cheese and olives or *ful madammas*. Arab bread is also the 'wrapper' used for

Baking* khubz arabi *in a traditional oven.

shawarmas and a handy pouch that holds Western-style sandwich fillings.

It is still possible to find small bakeries on suburban streets where traditional ovens produce the delicious, fresh bread for the neighbourhood. In the desert, bedouin prepare a dough and cook it on hot stones in the fire, later covering it with coals. Alternatively, they may cook the dough on a large, curved pan that has been inverted over the fire.

Originally, the bread was baked in large circles of fairly uniform diameter. Today, the bread comes in sizes large, medium, and small, adapted for use as *hors d'oeuvres* and pizza bases. Arab bread which has been brushed with oil, sprinkled with seasonings or orange rind, cut into bite-size strips or triangles, and baked in the oven makes a delicious snack. *See also* FOOD.

ARABIAN GULF. The Arabian Gulf (also referred to as the Persian Gulf or simply the Gulf) is a 610-kilometre stretch of water that flows into the Straits of Hormuz. It is bounded by Iraq on the north, Iran on the east, and Saudi Arabia and the Gulf countries of UAE, Qatar, and Oman on the west. The island of Bahrain is immediately off the east coast of Saudi Arabia in the Gulf.

The Arabian Gulf was once home to daring pirates, naval frigates, fishing boats, and wealthy merchant ships. Today, the only pirates are the entrepreneurs who try to overcharge the unwary for the rental of recreational equipment or boat rides! The Gulf remains an important trade lane, especially for the transport of Saudi Arabia's main export, oil. It is also a rich source of seafood, although severe over-fishing has reduced the once plentiful catches of shrimp and fish.

During the last century, pearling was one of the main sources of income of the Gulf's coastal villages. Today, the profession has virtually died out, partly because of increased opportunities in other fields and partly because of the prevalence of cultured pearls.

The relatively peaceful waters remain shallow for long distances offshore. The many shoals, reefs, uninhabited islands, and unspoiled coastlines of the Gulf make it an ideal habitat for a wide variety of migratory birds, turtles and marine life.

Although the underwater life is nowhere near as spectacular as that of the Red Sea off Saudi Arabia's west coast, the Gulf is nevertheless a popular place for diving enthusiasts. The waters provide exciting opportunities for discovering shipwrecks.

ARABIAN HORSE. An ancient bedouin legend poetically describes the origin of the Arabian horse: *And God took a handful of south wind and from it formed a horse, saying "I create thee, Oh Arabian. To thy forelock I bind victory in battle; on thy back I set a rich spoil and treasure in thy loins. I establish thee as one of the glories of the earth. I give thee flight without wings."* Legend also says that the Arabian's characteristic dished profile holds the blessings of Allah, its arched neck and high crest exemplify courage, and the high tail carriage symbolizes pride.

The exquisite Arabian is the horse in its purest form; they are the only true purebred. All popular modern breeds descend from this exceptional steed. The versatility of the Arabian allows it to distinguish itself in virtually all equine disciplines, including dressage, endurance, racing, jumping, and polo.

The noble qualities of the Arabian horse evolved in a harsh desert habitat that permitted only the strong to survive. Recognising and admiring these qualities, bedouin tribes began a programme of selective breeding. They kept oral records of lineages that went back hundreds of years.

The bedouin depended on their horses to carry heavy loads over long distances and to be swift and fearless in battle. Like the bedouin themselves, their animals had to be able to endure extended periods of sparse food and water supplies. In winter and spring, a non-working mare can survive as long as 40 days without water, getting sufficient moisture from vegetation. Bedouin often augment the grass, barley, and hay diets of their Arabians with treats such as camel milk, dates, sun-dried raw meat, and dried locusts. In addition to breeding and raiding, the bedouin increased the size of their herds by holding races: the loser forfeited his best horses to the winner.

Moghul rulers were importing Arabians to improve Indian breeds from the 13th century. Over time, the Arabian became legendary for its speed, stamina, intelligence, and loyalty. Early in the 18th century, the Arabian horse's rare combination of strengths attracted the attention of wealthy English sporting enthusiasts. New blood was needed to enhance the performance of the native English horse, which experts viewed as heavy, slow, and clumsy. Searching for suitable stock, the English breeders turned to the Arabian.

It is a credit to the

A prancing stallion shows all the suppleness and nobility of the purebred Arabian horse.

Arabians' resilience that they could adapt so well and so quickly to such an alien environment. To the amazed delight of the English, the new line produced remarkable results in the first generation of the new breed: the thoroughbred racehorse. Every one of today's thoroughbreds is a direct descendant of one of three sires: the Byerley Turk (an Arabian stallion captured from the Turks), the Godolphin Arabian, and the Darley Arabian.

Ironically, in the last two centuries, other countries devoted more attention to the Arabian horse than did Saudi Arabia. Today, that situation is reversed. Thanks to the considerable efforts and investment of a few devoted Saudi breeders, the Arabian horse has once again gained prominence in its homeland.

ARABIAN ORYX. *See* ORYX.

ARABIC. The true heritage of Arabia can be found in its language. In the nomadic culture, words could be carried without burden. In a harsh desert environment unconducive to the development of fine arts, the cultivation of language became an art form in itself. The immense power, beauty, and range of Arabic makes it one of history's greatest literary languages. Even today, poetry and eloquence are revered in the Saudi culture.

Spoken Arabic is not merely a tool for conceptualisation, it is a vehicle to create atmosphere and emotion. Add to this the rich vocabulary and the often ritual patterns of address and it is not hard to understand why it may take longer to express an idea in Arabic than in most other languages. Conversely, single Arabic words can encompass complex philosophical, even military, concepts.

Written Arabic, with its many graceful curves and swirls, lends itself to the art of calligraphy. The elegance of the script can be appreciated even by those who do not understand the meaning of the words.

Arabic is not an easy language to learn. In addition to the numerous dialects and extensive vocabulary, there are three families of Arabic: Classical, the language of the *Qur'an*; Standard Literary, used in the media and as a common communication between different dialects; and Spoken, the colloquial form distinct to each region. While geographic regions have their own dialects, such as Gulf or Egyptian, within these areas vocabulary and pronunciation can differ considerably. An Arab from one country cannot necessarily understand or be understood by someone from another country where Arabic is the main language, although they would both normally have recourse to the classical language if necessary.

The Arabic alphabet has 28 characters. Some of these represent different pronunciations of the same letter. A few of the sounds are strongly guttural and must be formed at the back of the throat, a considerable challenge for most students of the language.

All official correspondence with government bodies in Saudi Arabia must be in Arabic. *See also* CALLIGRAPHY; NUMBERS.

ARABIC COFFEE. Nothing symbolizes the tradition of hospitality in Arabia more than the ritual serving of coffee, a gesture signifying cordiality and welcome.

Although wild coffee plants originated in Ethiopia (Kaffa), it was in Arabia they were first cultivated in the 15th century. One legend attributes the discovery of coffee to

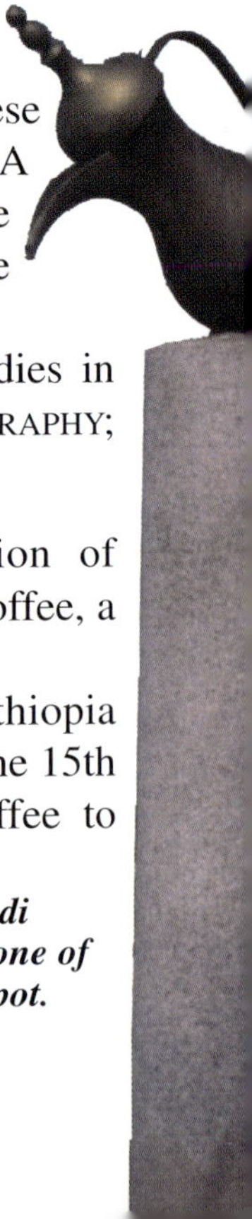

Coffee, and the ritual of serving it, is an integral part of Saudi culture. So much so that two of Jeddah's public sculptures (one of which is pictured right) portray the traditional Saudi coffee pot.

Arabic Coffee

Ingredients

- One small Arabic coffee cup of lightly browned coffee beans
- One small Arabic coffee cup of cardamon (*hail*)

Method

Coarsely grind the coffee beans. Fill a Saudi-style coffee pot* 3/4 full with water. Heat until the water boil.s. Add the ground coffee. Gently bring the mixture to the boil. Remove from heat and strain. Pour the filtered coffee into a second Saudi-style coffee pot and add the cardamon. For a more subtle flavour, use whole cardamon. Increase or decrease the quantity acording to taste. Place the pot on low heat. Serve just before the coffee begins to boil. Palm webbing or modern plastic imitation substitute placed at the spout prevents the grounds from being poured into the cups.

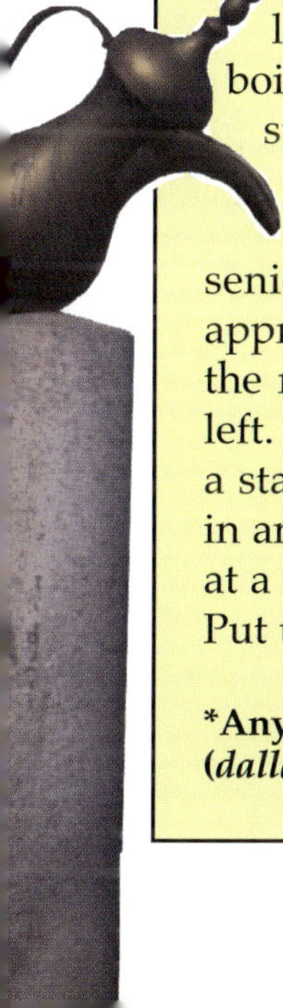

As a sign of respect, always serve the most senior guests first. If all the guests are of approximately the same age, serve the coffee from the right side and continue around the room to the left. Hold the pot with the left hand and the cups in a stack in the right hand. Excess cups can be placed in an inverted stack on the left thumb. Pour one cup at a time, letting each guest take his or her own cup. Put used cups at the bottom of the stack.

***Any pot can be used but the Saudi-style *qahwa* pot (*dallah*) (*left*) adds a traditional ambience to the procedure.**

Kaldi, a Yemeni goat-herd who, in AD 850, noticed the friskiness of his goats after they ate the red berries. It is not known why he progressed from chewing the berries to roasting and brewing them, but his breakthrough had a great impact on future generations. The full-bodied *Arabica* bean accounts for two-thirds of world coffee consumption.

Saudis consider cardamom a vital ingredient in coffee making. Either crushed or in pods, cardamom gives the brew a taste unique to this part of the world. A pinch of saffron may be included for extra flavour and colour. Some families also add their own blend of herbs and spices.

The yellowish coffee is generally drunk without sugar or milk from small bowl-shaped cups without handles. Guests should accept no more than three cups unless socializing with close friends. There is no obligation to drink the coffee but it is courteous to accept one cup in acknowledgement of the host's hospitality.

To indicate that he does not want any more coffee, the guest gently wobbles the cup back and forth or covers the cup with the palm of the hand before returning it to the server. Guests should always accept and return cups with their right hands. *See also* COFFEE RITUAL.

ARABIC NUMBERS. *See* NUMBERS.

ARCHAEOLOGICAL SITES. Many archaeological sites have been established and fenced off in Saudi Arabia but relatively few have been worked so far. Al-Fau, in the south, is a notable exception.

Because of the peninsula's legendary wealth and cultural achievements during the time of the trade routes, not to mention its religious impact on the world, the treasures and insights into the past that lie beneath Arabia's sands must surely be staggering.

One reason for the seeming lack of progress in archaeological digs in Saudi Arabia is the sensitivity towards pre-Islamic discoveries. Another factor has been that, until recently, an enthusiasm to embrace modernity has taken priority over interest in the past. The Kingdom's main cities and many smaller towns now have excellent museums devoted to regional discoveries, shedding light on periods from the Early Stone Age to the Islamic period.

Visitors to most sites, including some forts, require written permission from the Directorate-General of Antiquities and Museums in Riyadh. For tour groups, this permission is obtained by the tour company. Even with permission, it is not always possible to gain access to the site upon arrival: the guard may be away...for lunch or for the day...but it is usually worth persevering. *See also* AL-FAU; AL-JAWF; DIR'IYYAH; MADAIN SALEH; PETROGLYPHS; TARUT ISLAND.

ARCHITECTURE. Though the bedouin tent is viewed as the typical Arabian dwelling, the majority of today's population descends not from nomadic bedouin but from settled communities.

Houses were designed with privacy in mind as well as considerations of climate and location. In the west of Saudi Arabia particularly, designs were also influenced by itinerant cultures.

One of the most striking examples of this is in the small, southwestern province of Jizan where the climate in hot and humid. Here, in the coastal area of Tihama, one can still see haystack-like huts. Centuries ago, Africans travelled north to Arabia as traders and pilgrims. Many stayed and made a new life for themselves, primarily in the coastal plains which reminded them of their native lands. The Africans used the familiar local building materials of dried river reeds and mud plaster to recreate *rondavel* huts with thatched roofs similar to those they had left in Sudan and Ethiopia. This type of construction allows a continuous flow of air and prevents the heat building up by 'breathing' through the porous walls and the woven roof.

The interior mud-plastered walls are often whitewashed

This vividly decorated ceiling is typical of dwellings in the Tihama region.

and decorated in vivid primary colours. Geometric patterns may be painted onto the conical ceilings. An arched doorway forms the only opening. Despite the lack of windows, lighting is adequate when the door is open.

Yemeni influence can be seen in the designs of traditional houses of the foothills and escarpment of the Tihama. The tall buildings are made from either mud, stone, or a combination of the two. The thick walls provide a cool retreat in summer and a warm shelter during the cold winter months.

The height of the houses varies from the one- or two-storey structures frequently found in the Baha region, to the three- to five-storey houses for which the Asir is renowned.

In Saudi Arabia's mountainous regions of the Asir and Taif houses are typically tall, usually having between two and five storeys, and occasionally as many as nine storeys, and are built from stone rubble, mud, and slate. Tall houses meant more land available for farming. The tower structure also gave a measure of security in the event of attack.

In the Asir, where precipitation is high, it is not uncommon to see skillfully built mud and slate houses. Layers of slate protruding perpendicularly from the walls protect the mud structure from erosion and mean minimal maintenance. Inside, the walls, floors, ceilings, and stairs are a surprising riot of sharp, high-gloss colours that incorporate geometric patterns.

Less peaceful settlement came with the Turkish invasion of more than 350 years ago. The Turks introduced their building and decorating techniques. In the southwest regions, these are most evident in the remaining fortifications and garrisons.

Mashrabiyas or *rawshan*, probably influenced by Ottoman and Egyptian designs, are typical in the Jeddah-Taif region. These wooden, screened bay windows were decorative as well as functional. The small balconies with their lattice screens allow the occupants to see without being seen. *Mashrabiyas* also provide additional private space for families and refreshing ventilation. Supported by corbels, or timbers, protruding from a building's outer walls, some *mashrabiyas* boast exquisitely carved panels, cornices, eaves, and shutters.

The beautiful wooden doors and window shutters that stand in sharp

Mashrabiyas adorn the façade of this house in Jeddah.

contrast to usually stark façades have become collectors' items prized for their craft and creativity. Each region has its own distinctive style: brightly coloured geometric shapes painted onto burned or carved designs distinguish the doors and windows of the Najd; in the Eastern Province, ornate metalwork is the primary decoration on designs that reflect Mesopotamian, Persian, and Indian influences; the Hijaz, with its long, cosmopolitan history is a showcase of spectacularly carved doors; the doors of Asir, the Kingdom's most colourful province, are but a brief introduction to the distinctive and equally colourful interiors. In order to protect a family's privacy, front doors never directly face each other.

In hot, arid regions, such as Riyadh, Qassim, Makkah, and Madina, the traditional atrium adobe house is ideally suited to the climate. The courtyard provides both light and the movement of air. If the proportions of the atrium are correct, it will effectively keep the house cool during the day and warm at night. Atria also have the advantage of allowing the occupants to be outside yet private, privacy being an important feature in Muslim society.

The thick adobe construction insulates against the high summer temperatures and the cold desert nights. It is typical for these houses to be joined to each other, usually on three sides, thus providing further protection from the elements. The residential streets and walkways in adobe communities were traditionally the width of a loaded camel, providing welcome shade and respite from sand storms. Commercial streets were the width of two loaded camels. *See also* AL-FAISALIAH; WIND TOWER.

ARDHA. *See* DANCE.

ASIR. Asir is a province of exceptional scenery, untamed wilderness, and a cultural heritage as colourful as its varied vegetation. The Asiri welcome, *marhaban alf* (1,000 welcomes), reflects the friendliness of the people.

The word Asir means 'difficult', a most appropriate description for the geography of the region. Until recently, the deep wadis and steep mountains permitted only rough trails to impinge upon their domain. Travelling to the next village could take days and test even the most intrepid traveller. Construction in the late 1970s of the challenging Sha'ar Descent road was so demanding and dangerous that it required skilled mountain climbers to carry out the preliminary work. Although daunting to technology, this mighty statement of nature is precisely what attracts so many visitors to the area.

Asir's topography not only supports different forms of plant and animal life, but also a cross-section of cultures. It is an objective of officials to preserve the area's diverse customs, including traditional agricultural methods, local architecture, and artistic skills.

Natives of the foothills are mostly nomadic herders. In the highlands, sedentary communities dot the landscape. Fertile terraces hewn from the steep slopes grow grains, fruits, and vegetables. The oldest terraces date back more than 2,500 years. These mountain villages breed skilled goldsmiths, silversmiths, and weavers who carry on trades passed down through countless generations.

In the foothills and escarpment, centuries of driving rains and howling winds have carved deep and sometimes treacherous designs in the earth's façade. In this cooler climate, flora and fauna abound. Wildcats, ibex, and oryx roam the highlands in increasing numbers. An area of nine square kilometres is kept for the specific purpose of restocking rare, indigenous species which have become endangered or extinct in the Asir. As well, new strains are being introduced.

On Tuesdays in Abha, the capital, and Thursdays in the sister town of Khamis Mushayt, traders from the outlying districts congregate to sell their wares in the weekly markets. In these *suqs* visitors can see a clear illustration of the region's traditions and talents. These lively gatherings reflect both present-day customs and a life-style of generations long departed. Antique weaponry stirs images of a less peaceful past, while the wizened old men selling musical instruments present a more cultural aspect of the society. Foodstuffs indiscriminately tantalize the browser's senses of smell, sight, and taste. Here one finds large tins of tightly-packed, fleshy, sweet dates and a cornucopia of fruits and vegetables. Tribesmen wearing garlands of leaves in their hair *(right)* sell rare, wild honey from the Tihama and home-made *ghee* in dried kidskin containers. Locally woven baskets with colourful geometic designs and the wide-brimmed straw hats so characteristic of the region are particularly popular with foreign visitors.

Through Asir's Wadi Hali runs the most difficult stretch of the ancient incense route. Along these circuitous trails, camels laboured under their burdens of frankincense, myrrh, and other precious commodities bound for Europe and the Levant. Villagers still ply this route, although newer roads now take the bulk of the traffic.

One of the most intriguing villages for the tourist is Habala, also called the 'hanging village'. The name Habala comes from the Arabic word *habl* meaning 'rope'. Nestled at the base of a precipice surrounded by sheer cliffs, the war-weakened Qahtani tribe chose this virtually inaccessible valley for its home to escape from invading Turks and hostile tribes. These first settlers fixed a large peg into the top of a cliff, secured a strong rope, then lowered their livestock, personal belongings, provisions, and finally themselves down the 100-metre drop. Although no longer inhabited, the stone houses remain and the terraced fields which grew crops such as coffee, grains, and bananas, are still a flourishing green.

Another of the area's romantic stories revolves around a cone-shaped hill called Black Mountain or Queen of Sheba Mountain. According to legend, the Queen spent one year at the mountain on her way to see King Solomon at Ophir. On some of the large black stones which cover the hill, picture writing and rock carvings can be seen, adding a flavour of mystery to the tale. *See also* ABHA; ASIR NATIONAL PARK.

ASIR NATIONAL PARK. In order to preserve the beautiful landscape, flora, and fauna of the Asir, the Saudi government set aside 450,000 hectares of land and sea in 1976 to form the Asir National Park, the first such reserve in the Arabian peninsula.

An attractive Visitor Centre introduces guests to the vicinity. In the Centre's large auditorium a comprehensive slide presentation adds dimension to seven main rooms and exhibits. Each room displays its own theme on the region's natural or cultural background. The outdoor viewing platform with fixed telescopes allows a first-hand peek at the majesty which awaits guests on their tour of the park.

The park's perimeters encompass three distinct climatic zones: the sea and coastal areas, the foothills, and the escarpment. An area of nine square kilometres at Al-Jurrah is kept for the specific purpose of restocking species which have become endangered or extinct in the Asir. As well, entirely new strains of flora and fauna are being introduced.

So that the public can more fully participate in the pleasures of the reserve, park authorities have subtly developed selected areas. One of these is at Al-Sooda, the highest peak in the Kingdom. Strategic look-out points allow visitors to observe the surrounding bold assertion of nature.

This sector of substantial woodlands and verdant valleys receives more precipitation in a year than the rest of the Kingdom combined. The moist air from the Red Sea cools as it rises to Al-Sooda's lofty altitude of 3,200 metres. Ensuing clouds gather and can build into brief but brutal storms, causing serious flooding. Normally gentle streams which course their way through mountain cleavages turn into devastating torrents during heavy rains. Terracing, dams, and forests of juniper trees help prevent some of the inevitable erosion resulting from such furious displays of the elements. Most afternoons a thick fog rolls in from the coastal plains far below.

Other developed locales include oasis-like Al-Dalaghan, surrounded by rocks and mountains and fish-filled ponds, and Al-Qara'ah with its hiking trails, football fields, and superb viewing of soaring birds. There are also camping sites at the Red Sea.

Water and electricity services at the various camping grounds, beautifully located picnic spots, playgrounds, beaches, and foot trails contribute to the visitor's overall enjoyment of the park. These designated sections have well-maintained public toilets and, in some spots, food concessions. Yet there is no hint of commercialism. Park officials aim to preserve the area's cultural customs, including traditional agricultural methods, local architecture, and art forms.

Park notices ask guests to leave the area in the same condition as they find it: *Please take only pictures and leave only footprints.*

ASTROLOGICAL/ZODIAC CALENDAR. In addition to the *hejira* calendar and the Gregorian calendar, Saudis follow a solar astrological calendar. This corresponds to the Gregorian calendar but months are referred to by their zodiac names: Aquarius, Pisces, Aries, Taurus, Gemini, Cancer, Leo, Virgo, Libra, Scorpio, Sagittarius, and Capricorn. The national budget and school holidays follow the zodiac calendar.

B

B

BABOON. Any visitor along the roads between Taif and the southwestern regions of Saudi Arabia is sure to encounter the cheeky, pink-bottomed baboons (*Papio hamadryas*) that pester humans for food. It is kinder to resist the temptation. Apart from the facts that they lose the ability (and inclination) to fend for themselves, or that donated food may not be good for them, particularly bold baboons usually have to be shot in order to prevent them from harming unsuspecting visitors. Although their antics can be entertaining, these powerfully built creatures can also be dangerous. Humans are well advised to keep their distance.

The animals travel in bands of 12-20, and as many as 50, males and females. Unlike the African variety of the species, the Arabian females remain with one partner for life; males select a number of females with whom to mate. One or two young are born after a six-month gestation period. Shortly after birth, babies are strong enough to cling to their mothers. In case of danger, mother and infant can thus keep pace with the rest of the troop.

The long, dog-like muzzles contrast sharply with the animal's small ears and sunken eyes. Males are distinguished by their shaggy silver manes. When baboons walk or run, they raise their long tails vertically, revealing bright pink bottoms.

Omnivorous baboons forage in wadis and hillsides on fruit, grasses, roots, lizards, beetles, butterflies, and even scorpions. They supplement their diets whenever possible with donations from picnickers. Rubbish dumps also attract their attention. This has resulted in serious problems of trying to manage the increasingly aggressive troops.

BAHARAT. This mixed spice is one of the most popular in the Arabian peninsula. Most families have their own special blend. *Baharat* can be added to almost any savoury dish to enhance the flavour. Common ingredients are nutmeg, black pepper, coriander, cloves, cinnamon, cardamom, paprika, and chili.

BAKSHEESH. Foreigners usually refer to *baksheesh* as a complimentary gift to accompany a purchase. Shopkeepers may offer a small something voluntarily or the buyer may request it in order to confirm a sense of having made a good bargain. To Saudis, however, the word actually has negative connotations of bribery.

BANKING. *See* ISLAMIC BANKING.

BARGAINING. The skill of bargaining seems inherent in the Arab personality. Saudis greet the prospect of bargaining with enthusiasm and see it as a chance to match wits. Reaching a favourable agreement is a game they play to win, but with as much proficiency and good grace as possible.

During the opening moves of exchanging greetings, a good negotiator establishes eye contact in an effort to appraise the 'opponent' – who of course uses the same techniques to try to gain advantage. Each looks *into* the other's eyes, searching for signs of strength or weakness.

In order to bargain from a position of strength, it is essential to know the value of the item being negotiated. If this is not possible then it is safe to assume that the quoted price has been inflated at least 20 per cent.

Good bargainers know when to smile at a preposterous bid, when to express shock or dismay, when to pretend to walk away, and when really to walk away. Most importantly, they do not take themselves or the negotiations so seriously that they forget to enjoy the experience. In successful bargaining, both parties should feel satisfied with the deal.

After the price has been agreed, the effort is often rewarded with a complimentary gift called *baksheesh*, symbolizing the cementing of friendship. Whether offered by the vendor or requested by the purchaser, it makes the deal a little sweeter. Saudis are not just good at negotiating, they are also adept at commercial psychology! *See also* BAKSHEESH.

BEDOUIN. Although Arabia has always had large settled populations, in the Western mind it is the bedouin tribesmen who are most closely associated with the peninsula.

The word 'bedouin' is actually the French version of the plural of the Arabic word *bedu*, which itself is the plural of *badawi* meaning 'desert dweller'. All bedouin tribes can trace their descent from Shem, the son of Noah. To the romantic imagination, these noble warriors who survive in the harshest conditions make sedentary communities seem dull and pampered in comparison. The reality, however, is that their lives represent a relentless battle with nature.

The bedouin count their wealth in livestock. Camel raids were therefore an important and frequent routine in the past. Successful raids enhanced wealth and, consequently, status. The more successful raids a tribe carried out, the more prosperous and powerful it became.

There has always existed a symbiotic relationship between the settled and migrant populations. Bedouin tribes rely on towns for tools, weapons, jewellery, and basic supplies. Because of their itinerant lifestyles, bedouins played an important role in the transport of food and other commodities between settled communities. This source of income was supplemented by activities such as providing protection to agricultural areas, lesser tribes, and caravans which passed through their territory. Today the need for these services has all but disappeared. Nevetheless, the bedouin remain pastoralists, although their lifestyles are enhanced by pickup trucks, water tankers, gas burners, and electric generators.

Bedouin tribes were generally divided between those that herded camels and those with sheep and goats. Of the two, camels were the more prestigious; camel-based tribes tended to look down on those who had sheep and goats. Changing times, however, have dictated that, in order to survive, many of the camel-based tribes must diversify and also herd sheep. The fast-growing settled population has meant an increase in the demand for mutton as a food source. Motor-driven transportation, on the other hand, has seen the decline of the camel which was once essential for the transport of trade goods and the movement of people.

The need for so many tribes to turn to breeding sheep has resulted in an increase in semi-sedentary populations. Sheep

B

At one with their surroundings, a bedouin and his camels brave the scorching midday sun.

cannot survive as long as camels without water, so they cannot travel on long migrations through the desert. Because sheep are now more profitable than camels, the bedouin can afford to buy feed, further reducing the need to seek distant pastures. These subtle changes have meant that the bedouin are no longer self-reliant. Increasingly, they depend on an income to pay for the upkeep on their trucks and buy fodder. Schooling and job opportunities that provide a steady wage are further attractions to adapt to a settled life. Nevertheless, in many families, there remains a conflict between abandoning old, respected ways and adjusting to the demands of modern society. Their traditional resourcefulness and flexibility play a vital role in the success of their adaptability.

Bedouin honour is legendary. Through vagaries of nature or battle, all wealth may be lost. Only honour and reputation remain under the control of the individual. These are the bedouin's most precious assets. Their importance is instilled from early childhood. Honour and disgrace are borne not only by the individual but by the entire tribe, becoming a blessing or a burden to successive generations. A woman's honour is protected at all costs to spare the shame of the family. A female found guilty of sexual indiscretion might still face death at the hands of her father or male guardian.

In warfare, the bedouin followed strict rules of engagement. Women and children were inviolate; no matter how bloody the battle, the women and children were always left with a tent and the necessities for cooking. The object of a raid was usually to acquire camels. Other livestock and property were normally ignored, and no raiding was allowed between midnight and dawn.

Many bedouin traditions are shared by the general population. The exceptional hospitality, for example, for which Arabs are renowned, stems from the basic rule of the desert: protection was granted to whomever came to an encampment, whether friend, foe, or stranger. During the first three days, the visitor was under no obligation to reveal his name or any other personal details, nor would he be asked. Travellers were welcome as an important source of information regarding rains, pasture lands, and the activities of other tribes.

Although the nomadic lifestyle is declining, modern society has much to learn from these highly adaptable people who consider honour their most prized possession. *See also* TRIBES.

BEDOUIN JEWELLERY. The heavy, ornate styles of bedouin jewellery have an exotic and ethnic appeal that has recently made it a popular fashion accessory in countries far removed from Arabian deserts.

The distinctive silver pieces are called 'bedouin' jewellery because they were made *for* the bedouin, not by them. Silversmiths, based in communities through which the bedouin passed, usually associated themselves with a particular tribe and designed exclusively for their tastes and needs.

Necklaces are often heavy and extremely large, covering the entire upper chest. Ankle and arm bracelets, too, are large, thick pieces. Some can weigh as much as 200 grams. Bedouin women also like to adorn themselves with ear, nose, and finger rings, sometimes wearing a ring on every finger. Various types of silver head ornaments and belts form part of traditional collections.

A silver anklet.

Some of the silver pieces might be embossed or filigreed; others are decorated with semi-precious stones, particularly turquoise, agate, amber, coral, and carnelian. Red stones are the most popular, although turquoise, too, is common. Coins, such as the Maria Theresa thaler, frequently served as decoration on jewellery. The older and rarer the coins, the more prestige this bestowed on the wearer, for it meant that the person who gave her the jewellery valued her highly.

An interesting feature of bedouin jewellery is the fact that the many hanging baubles – coins, balls, beads – serve the purpose of announcing the approach of the wearer with a rhythmical jingling sound. This is useful in a society where men and women are segregated. The audible warning allows men time to disappear discreetly.

Despite the fact that the recently produced bedouin jewellery often suffers from fake gems and decreasing silver content, the pieces continue to be handmade and, as such, often show quality workmanship in details such as intricate filigree work. Within the past 40 years gold jewellery has become popular but it is still the rustic silver that is so closely associated with bedouin designs.

Traditionally, when a woman died, her jewellery was melted down. It is considered unsuitable for a new bride to have second-hand jewellery. This explains why there are relatively few pieces of authentic old bedouin jewellery. *See also* JEWELLERY.

BEDOUIN TENT. In Saudi Arabia the bedouin say, *A man's tent is like a god's temple*. The sentiment is understandable, coming from a people whose shelter can mean the difference between life and death. The simplicity of the distinctive bedouin tent (*bayt al sha'ar* – house of hair) is designed to suit a pastoral-nomadic lifestyle. A wise Arab proverb says,

The secret is in the people who live in the house and not in the house itself. Although the tents may be elementary in structure, they are nevertheless immensely practical and suited to the climate.

The tent fabric is coarsely woven in long strips from black or brown goat hair, though camel hair, wool, or cotton may also be used. The loose weave allows the heat to disperse in the summer months. During the rainy season, the fabric swells to close the holes. This and the naturally oily yarn make the tents moderately waterproof. The woven strips are sewn together with strong thread made from black goat's hair.

Two or three longitudinal rows of poles (depending on whether they are northern or southern Arabian nomads) support the fabric, the centre poles standing taller than the outer rows. Wooden pegs and hemp ropes stretch the sides and serve as fastenings against desert winds. The open side of the tent always faces away from the wind; when the wind changes direction the tent is repositioned. In hot weather, flaps in the front and back of the tent are raised to allow a circulation of air; in cold weather, all the flaps are closed.

Black is the traditional colour of the outside of the tents. Inside, the cloth walls and the partitions separating the men's section, the family section, and the cooking area are colourfully woven and decorated with a variety of geometric patterns. Sometimes the women's section incorporates the cooking and storage areas. The much smaller men's section also serves as the reception area for guests. It is always at the east end of the tent, irrespective of the tent's direction.

BEDOUIN WEAVING. Bedouin women spin camel, sheep, or goat hair on a simple drop spindle. This thread is either used to stitch woven strips together or is woven on a horizontal ground loom. Because of the migratory lifestyle of the

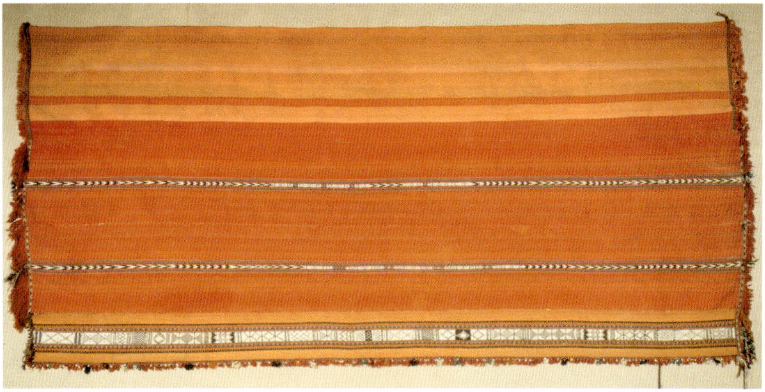

A bedouin rug woven from dyed sheep's wool.

bedouin, looms have to be easily portable. They are normally no wider than the length of a forearm, a size which severely restricts the size of weavings.

Because the looms were constantly being erected and dismantled, weavings were often irregularly shaped: incomplete pieces could not always be stretched back to their original positions. These irregularities, however, confirm a weaving's authentic bedouin heritage and, as such, give it added value. As well, the designs always have imperfections woven into them. This reflects the Muslim beleif that nothing is perfect except Allah.

Although natural colours are often used, especially for tents, colours brighten up accessories such as animal trappings, rugs, and tent wall hangings. In former times, these colours came from local plants such as madder, indigo, and henna, and minerals such as iron oxide. Today, chemical shades are more commonly used. Red is the predominant colour in bedouin weavings.

Because Islam does not allow the portrayal of human and animal forms, designs are almost always geometric.

BELOTE. This hugely popular card game is played throughout the Kingdom. Similar to bridge but with less complicated bidding, the game is played with the 2s and 6s removed from the pack. The first player to accumulate a minimum of 501 point is the winner. This takes several hands to achieve.

BETROTHAL. Courtship as it is known in the West does not exist in Saudi society. Here, with few exceptions, marriages are arranged by female family members. Traditional Arabs believe that marriage should foster love rather than be a result of love.

In former times, it was important to maintain the strength of the family and prevent dilution of both blood and assets. The ideal marriage was considered to be between first cousins. An old Arab expression says, *Marrying a strange woman is like drinking water from an earthenware bottle; marriage with a cousin is like a drink from a dish – you are aware of what you drink.* The offspring of close friends provide an alternate choice. Recent studies indicate a growing trend for young men and women to marry outside their circle of relatives. This is largely due to increased awareness about the health risks associated with consanguinity.

The closest adult male relative (as long as he is Muslim) or a reliable member of the community ensures that the proposed union will not bring dishonour to the families. After the prospective partners have passed scrutiny by both families, the man's relatives make a proposal. Islam does not allow forced marriages. The silence of a virgin indicates both modesty and consent. Widows and divorcées must agree to the marriage verbally.

Once all the initial discussions have been completed

successfully, the potential groom officially asks the father or guardian of the potential bride for her hand in marriage. Acceptance of the offer signals the engagement (*khutbah*) of the couple and is cause for celebration. The *khutbah* may be the first time that the young man and woman have ever seen each other. Their formal engagement means that the couple can meet whenever they like, as long as they are chaperoned.

Saudis consider it a duty to marry but there are certain restrictions on the choice of partner. If possible, the social and economic status of the couple should be equal or within a prescribed range. In some families, to marry outside the accepted limits is cause for ostracism. In any match, the husband must keep his wife in the style to which she was accustomed – or better.

As desirable as social equality may be, religious equality in marriage is even more important, especially among the *Shi'ite* sect. Muslims may marry only other Muslims or 'people of the book', i.e. Christians or Jews. Inter-faith marriage is not encouraged, but when it occurs, the non-Muslim spouse may not inherit from the Muslim spouse. In such cases, conversion to Islam is common. Under no circumstances may a Muslim woman marry a non-Muslim man, although a Muslim man may marry a non-Muslim woman. In this case, the non-Muslim woman can retain her own religion but their children must be brought up as Muslims.

Muslim men are permitted to have four wives at any one time but the women cannot be related to each other. Islam obliges the man to treat each wife equally in every way. For many reasons, not least financial ones, polygamy is becoming less common in Saudi society.

Adult widows or divorced women have slightly more freedom than first-time brides. They may choose their own husbands and negotiate the marriage contract. However, if they are pregnant, they must give birth before remarrying. While it is considered commendable to marry a widow, marriage to a widower or divorced man with children is less desirable for a woman's first marriage. *See also* MARRIAGE; MARRIAGE CONTRACT.

BISHT. Throughout the year as a mark of prestige, or during the winter for added warmth, a full-length cloak of cream, brown, or black wool or camel hair called a *bisht* or *mishlah* is worn over the *thobe*, the traditional attire for Saudi men. Openings in the side seams just below the shoulders allow the wearer's arms to protrude. Usually, however, the cloak rests on the shoulders and the right side is neatly tucked under the left arm.

Fabrics range from unadorned coarse wool to beautifully woven gold braided garments of the finest wool or camel hair. The best materials are imported from Japan and Europe and sewn in Saudi Arabia. The patterns of gold braid edging the garment are what principally distinguish the best from the ordinary *bisht.* Because it is so expensive to buy the more elegant *bisht* or *mishlah*, many men choose to rent them for occasions such as weddings and special ceremonies.

Although the loose, flowing style makes the *bisht* look like a one-size-fits-all garment, each *bisht* is tailored to fit the wearer. Interestingly, they are not shortened at the hemline but at a seam which runs horizontally at approximately knee level. *See also* FARWA; GHUTRAH; IGAAL; SIRWAAL; TAQIYAH; THOBE.

BURAYDAH. Located about 330 kilometres north of Riyadh, this main city of the Qassim area is the heartland of religious conservatism in Saudi Arabia. Here, even foreign women are forced to veil and wear an *abaya*.

Buraydah is famous for its masons and builders. When craftsmen are required in other parts of the country to restore old buildings, it is usually the men of Buraydah who are summoned. This was the best constructed of the old mud towns of Najd. Today, much of the old architectural heritage has disappeared but enough of the beautiful walls and houses remain to justify the claim of excellence. The wonderful tamarisk and iron-studded doors are finer here than anywhere else.

BURIAL. In order not to prolong the anguish of the bereaved, Muslim burials take place as soon as possible after death. The body should be laid to rest before sunset on the day of the death but increasing bureaucracy often makes this impossible. Administrative procedure requires the identity of the deceased, the establishment of the next of kin, and a medical diagnosis of the cause of death before the body can be released for burial. Death in suspicious circumstances necessitates police intervention, inevitably resulting in further delays.

Upon issuance of the burial order, the body is washed, scented, and wrapped in white, unseamed cloth. A *surah* from the *Qur'an* is read before mourners go to the grave. Close male friends or family members carry the bier. Custom prevents women from accompanying the deceased to the grave in order to avoid emotional outbursts.

When a woman is buried, only her *mahram* (male family members whom she cannot marry) can uncover her face before lowering her body into the grave. The grave itself, which bears no headstone, is aligned in the direction of Makkah. In general, personal possessions of the deceased are not treasured as heirlooms, but are disposed of. *See also* DEATH; MOURNING.

BURQA. This heavily decorated, stiff mask ties at the back of the head, leaves the forehead bare, and has openings for the eyes. It is worn mostly by women in southwestern tribes. *See also* ABAYA; TARHA; WOMEN'S DRESS.

C

C

CALLIGRAPHY. *Purity of writing proceeds from purity of heart.* This statement by Sultan Ali (d. 1520) refers to Islam's most highly esteemed art, calligraphy.

The term 'calligraphy' derives from ancient Greek words meaning 'beautiful' and 'drawing'. Arabic calligraphy, with its natural flow of letters, is writing raised to an art form and actually represents the foundation of Islamic arts. Fine

A marble inscription in ornamental Kufi script.

examples of calligraphy can be found incorporated into almost all materials, whether they be carved, woven, or written, as sophisticated art or a simple means of communication.

The Arabic calligrapher works with a *qalam*, a traditional reed pen whose nib is cut at an angle. This permits thick downward strokes and fine upward strokes, with many possibilities to graduate the thickness of lines. The idiosyncrasies of Arabic script, such as its lack of capital letters and the fact that some letters cannot be joined to others, lend themselves to the graceful strokes of calligraphy.

To a large extent, Islam has been responsible for the esteem accorded written Arabic. For Muslims, not only the meaning but the actual words revealed by God to his prophet Muhammad are sacred. The art of copying the *Qur'an*, the recorded word of God, therefore became a meritorious act and inspired talented calligraphers to create works of immense visual imagination using quotations from the *Qur'an*. Islam brought a widespread rejection of the depiction of humans and animals. Instead, efforts were devoted to the aesthetic presentation of letters, resulting in a superb expression of visual art.

One of the major characteristics of Arabic architecture is its fascination with the incorporation of calligraphy. The text is first written on paper and then transferred to tiles for firing and glazing or stone for carving. Sometimes inscriptions are woven into geometric designs; other times proclamations might cover a building's or monument's façade.

Many scripts have evolved through the ages, some more difficult to read than others. The *Kufi* script, developed during the classical period of Islam, is considered the most majestic. Its rigidly angular letters are well suited for carving into wood, stone, or metal. From *kufi* evolved the

C

elegantly cursive *nashki* script. The elaborate *diwani* style, devised by the Ottomans, is a ceremonial calligraphy. Some of the other scripts in contemporary use include *thuluth* and *tawqi'*. All the variations have in common a special beauty that can be appreciated even by people who do not understand what is written.

CAMEL. Few things are more closely associated with Saudi Arabia than the one-humped dromedary camel. Bedouins refer to the camel as God's gift, *ata allah*, for without this sturdy beast they would not have had such mobility through the harsh desert terrain. As well as transportation, camels were a source of meat and milk, their dung provided fuel for camp fires, the hair was woven into fabric for tents and accessories, hides were crafted into containers and other leather-based necessities, and the potent urine was used medicinally, including as a treatment against hair lice. Wilfred Thesiger, the writer and explorer, claimed, *It is not hunger or thirst that frightens the Bedouin. It is the possible collapse of their camels that haunts them. If that happens, death is certain.*

Domesticated for more than 4,000 years, camels were instrumental in transporting commercial goods up and down Arabia's famous overland trade routes. They were directly responsible for allowing early Arabian tribes to engage in trade activities throughout Arabia and the Levant.

The camel is admirably adapted to survive in Arabia's harsh environment, where temperatures can reach 54ºC. A double row of long eyelashes protects the camel's eyes from blowing sand. A thin, supplemental eyelid can move from side to side to get rid of sand particles that might slip through. Camels can continue walking in sand storms by closing the third eyelid and keeping the other two open. Broad, protruding ridges of bone above each eye help shield the eyes from bright sunlight.

Acute hearing is belied by the camel's relatively small ears. The size and the fact that they are lined with fur make it difficult for sand to get in. Large, muscular nostrils that can be opened and closed at will prevent sand from blowing up the camel's nose. Thick, fleshy lips and strong teeth enable the camel to eat thorny vegetation as well as less challenging dates, grass, and grains. The tough lips are so adept at gathering food that the camel seldom has to lose precious moisture by sticking out its tongue.

When grazing is sparse, the fat stored in the hump nourishes the camel. As this supply is drawn upon, the hump shrinks and becomes flabby. It returns to normal when the camel finds plentiful grazing again.

One of the most significant features that allows the camel to survive is its ability to avoid water loss so well that it can

Camels lie facing the sun, minimising heat absorption by exposing the least possible body area to direct sunlight.

go for as long as six months (during the winter) without drinking, deriving the water it needs from its fodder, providing this is sufficiently fresh and verdant. The camel has two special capabilities: a unique metabolism that allows it to consume as much as 100 litres in just ten minutes and store the intake in the bloodstream (*not* in the hump); and the ability to raise its body temperature tolerance in order to conserve body fluids.

Camels make excellent use of their food: passing food back and forth through four stomach chambers maximises nourishment and minimises waste. New protein is created by recycling urea through the liver,. Urine output is therefore extremely limited.

Over long distances, camels can outrun horses. A working camel can travel approximately 40 kilometres per day walking at a comfortable three-four kilometres/hour. Racing camels can gallop 20 kilometres/hour. Unloaded, a mature camel can keep a pace of 13 kilometres/hour for up to 18 hours. Because the camel moves both feet on the same side of its body at the same time, the gait resembles a rolling motion. Broad, leathery, padded, two-toed feet support the camel in soft sand.

The camel's powerful legs allow it to carry burdens up to 450 kilos, although the average cargo weight is more in the region of 150 kilos. In order to allow time to recuperate from such heavy loads, camels work for only six to eight months a year.

Because camels are kept primarily for milk, herds comprise a majority of females. On rare occasions when camels are slaughtered for food, such as weddings or in honour of a visiting dignitary, males are invariably selected. Only the more docile female camels are used for riding. Riding camels are never used for breeding.

The gestation period is 13 months. Camels reach maturity at five years of age and, on average, live for 40 years.

CAMEL BAG. These large, colourfully woven bags come in pairs, connected by two long woven cables so that they can hang on either side of the camel's hump. They are used to pack the items being transported by the camels. Patterns and colours vary by region. Collectors like to hang them on the wall for decoration or stuff them for use as large floor cushions.

CAMEL BRANDS. Camels may be branded with several marks (*wasm*). This identifies the tribe, sub-tribe, and, on occasion, the individual who owns the camel.

CAMEL HAIR. Camels shed their coats each spring, yielding as much as 2.25 kilos of strong, warm wool. Internationally, this is valued for high-quality fabrics and artists' brushes. Bedouin weave the moulted hair into fabric for tents, rugs and other utilitarian items. Tents in Saudi Arabia are traditionally black; rugs can be a blend of the many colours of camel hair, from white to various colours of brown, to black. Camel hair cannot be dyed.

CAMEL MILK. This vital source of nutrition for bedouin tribes is normally drunk while still warm and frothy. The beverage is known to be high in potassium, iron, and vitamin C but low in fat and lactose. It is now sold commercially in Saudi supermarkets. Although healthier for humans than cow's milk, camel milk is an acquired taste for most Western palates.

The quality of the milk depends on the fodder. Years of plentiful rainfall result in better pastures, which produce better milk. When conditions are good, one camel can yield up to 19 litres each day. The best milk comes from a camel that has given birth for the first time.

Before being able to milk a camel, the calf must first stimulate the flow. Camels should be milked twice a day.

CAMEL MEAT. This somewhat chewy, slightly gamey-flavoured meat is considered a delicacy. Normally, only males are killed for food; females are kept for milk and transportation. Young male camels provide the most tender meat. For the urban shopper, various cuts can now be found in supermarkets. Although it would make sense to rear camels for meat in this arid land, sales of camel meat still fall far behind beef, chicken, and lamb.

CAMEL RACE. This sport no doubt began almost as soon as more than one camel had been domesticated long ago. Stakes in the races could be high, with the loser forfeiting his best camels to the winner.

Camel racing today is big business. Animals are specially bred for speed and stamina. A good racing camel can cost a small fortune. In order to minimise the load and thereby increase the chance of winning, boys as young as four years old serve as jockeys.

In the principal towns, the races begin about 50 kilometres out in the desert. Competitors then race to the finish line on the outskirts of town where the officiating dignitary bestows prizes. Nowadays, this is often a water tanker truck and cash.

The desert stretch has, in many towns and cities, been replaced by a purpose-built oval race track, similar to those used by horses but often with tall railings demarkating each of the lanes. Trying to get a race started can be chaotic and frustrating as the stubborn-minded beasts refuse to cooperate, get in the wrong lanes, or get their necks caught under the rails. It's an event only for those with patience. The King's Camel Race, held each year at Janadriyyah, (outside Riyadh) during the famous festival, is the largest in the world, with more than 1,000 camels participating.

C

CAMEL SADDLE. The rather cumbersome looking camel saddle is composed of a wooden frame that sits on the camel's hump. The northern Arabian version has a front and rear pommel between which is placed a padded cushion. The rider sits towards the front of the hump and positions his left leg around the front pommel.

The much smaller southern Arabian model has no pommels. The design requires the rider to sit at the back of the hump and necessitates a good sense of balance.

Bedouin steer the camel with reins attached to a halter on the camel's muzzle or with a rope connected to a ring in the animal's nostril.

CAMEL SPIDER. These 8-legged creatures are of the order *Solifugae*, meaning 'run from the sun', an appropriate description of their nocturnal habits. Although they do not actually belong to the arachnid family, their close resemblance to spiders and the fact that they often hide beneath camel saddles have given them their name. They are also referred to as 'wind scorpions', another misnomer.

Camel spiders can grow to the size of a man's hand. One of the most distinctive features of the camel spider is its enormous – and multiple – jaws. Two top jaws and two bottom jaws work independently to saw and mash its prey to manageable pulp. The males have a pair of long, hairy pedipalps protruding from the head region. Their sensitivity to odours helps the males to find females. The pedipalps are used in the mating ritual to stroke the female into a trance. This minimises the risk of the female turning on her mate and eating him. Although camel spiders have no stingers and are not poisonous, their unusually large mandibles allow them to take nasty

bites out of their prey. They first anaesthetise the victim and then dine. Their preferred diet is moths and other insects, easily caught in the light of the camp fire, lizards, beetles and even other camel spiders. These voracious eaters are extremely fast and usually catch their meals on the run.

CARDAMOM. Cardamom is one of the most ancient and most valued of spices. Either crushed or in pods, cardamom gives Arabic coffee its distinctive taste. Taken before a meal, cardamom prepares the stomach lining to accept food; after a meal, it aids digestion. Cardamom is also used to cleanse the breath, particularly after eating garlic. The seeds can be chewed or ground; pods are not eaten but are added whole to rice or stews for flavour.

Cardamom is indigenous to India and Sri Lanka, from where the spice was originally introduced to Arabia. Today, most of the Arab world's supply comes from Guatemala, the world's foremost exporter of the spice. Saudi Arabia is the largest consumer of cardamom.

CAUSEWAY. *See* KING FAHD CAUSEWAY.

CHILDBIRTH. The birth of the first child often comes within a year of marriage. Some newlyweds wait a little longer to start a family but they are still in the minority.

The festive occasion of childbirth is marked by the slaughter of a sheep in thanksgiving. Family and friends congratulate the new mother in the hospital and present her with gifts. One week after the child's birth, the infant is given a name and, if a boy, is circumcised. The parents receive special recognition with the new term of address *Om* (mother) or *Abu* (father) preceding the first-born son's name. Occasionally this applies instead to the birth of a first daughter (until the birth of the first son).

CITIES. Saudi Arabia's main cities are: Abha, Al-Khobar, Buraydah, Dammam, Dhahran, Hail, Jeddah, Jubail, Madinah, Makkah, Riyadh, Tabuk, Taif, and Yanbu. Many of these have developed or expanded substantially as a result of the oil industry. Consequently, most of the infrastructure is relatively recent. The population explosion has also contributed to the growth of Saudi cities where young people flock for education or job opportunities. *See also individual entries.*

CLIMATE. Arid is the term which best describes Saudi Arabia, although not all areas of the country suffer from extreme dry spells to the same extent. A monsoon influence in the Kingdom's mountainous southwestern province of Asir brings seasonal rainfall that averages 30-50 centimetres per annum. The country on the whole, however, averages less than 12 centimetres which occurs as a result of perhaps only a couple of downpours. In the Empty Quarter (*Rub Al-Khali*), the wide expanse of desert that stretches across the southeastern quarter, it may be as much as 10 years between rains.

Although the summer temperatures can be excessively high during the day, on occasion rising above 50ºC, evenings are comparatively cool. The thermometer seldom drops below 0ºC and often hovers in the vicinity of 14ºC-23ºC. The exceptions are in the north and in the higher altitudes where is can go below freezing, with occasional snow and ice. The abrupt decrease in evening temperatures makes the desert decidedly cold, requiring camp fires and warm clothing. The high humidity of the coastal regions – between 85 and 100 per cent – sharply contrasts with the extreme dryness of the interior.

Seasonal sandstorms are a feature throughout much of the country. These are produced by the *shamaal*, a forceful northwest wind that typically blows during the late spring and early summer. The Eastern Province also experiences the *kauf*, a southerly wind that signals increased temperatures and humidity.

C

COFFEE. *See* ARABIC COFFEE.

COFFEE RITUAL. Until recently, the preparation of coffee remained virtually unchanged throughout the centuries. Today, in offices and many urban homes, the method has been modified to meet the requirements of a faster-paced lifestyle with an emphasis on convenience. Yet the practice survives recognizably intact.

In the most traditional settings, green beans are lightly roasted over a fire in a long-handled, ladle-like utensil called a *mahmasa*. In order to keep the beans from becoming too dark, the *mahmasa* is gently turned and kept away from the flame and the roasting beans are stirred with an equally long-handled implement (*yad al mahmasa*) with a broad, flat end. When the beans begin to glow, they are placed in a wooden coffee box or tray (*mubarrad*) about 15-20 centimetres long and with a partially covered funnel opening at the narrower end.

The cooled beans are then coarsely and rhythmically ground in a mortar, or *nijr*, made from wood, stone, or brass. The ringing music from the *nijr,* distinctive to each tribe, invites anyone within earshot to come for coffee.

Water is placed in a pelican-beaked pot called a *dallah*. The ground coffee is added and brought to the boil. The vital ingredient of cardamom, and perhaps saffron and other spices, is added to the brew which is then brought to the boil once again. Finally, the steaming aromatic liquid is ready to serve. A sprig of dried palm webbing (*leefah*) placed in the spout is an ancient method of filtration which prevents the grounds and spices from entering the cups. *See also* ARABIC COFFEE.

COMPOUND. Because of the great disparity between Saudi culture and those of other countries, most foreign companies choose to house their employees in compounds. This allows residents the freedom to follow their own traditions without causing offence to their Saudi hosts.

Compounds vary in size, from two or three villas to as many as 300. Smaller compounds often have individual entrances for each house. Otherwise, cars enter through a security gate. In the more luxurious compounds, facilities compare favourably with those of the finest resorts: private swimming pools, golf courses, riding stables, health clubs, restaurants, and other amenities.

CONSULTATIVE COUNCIL. This traditional method of governing was restructured by King Fahd in 1992 and inaugurated in 1993. Known in Arabic the *Majlis As-Shura*, the Consultative Council's primary purpose is to advise the King on matters of policy and planning. The several groups within the framework of the Council sit regularly to study questions relating to politics, economics, education, and other national concerns. The Council works indirectly with the Cabinet to issue laws.

The Council President and 60 members are selected for a four-year period by the King from a cross-section of citizens throughout the country. The combined talents of businessmen, educators, former government officials, and other professionals ensure a balanced input. Each member must be well qualified, have a good reputation, and be a Saudi national, not just by birth but also by origin. *See also* GOVERNMENT.

COUNCIL OF MINISTERS. In 1953, the Council of Ministers was formed as one way to cope with the problems of rapid modernization as well as tribal and regional differences. This represented the first step towards a national administrative system.

The Council exercises both legislative and executive powers and is headed by the King, followed by the First Deputy Prime Minister (the Crown Prince). In addition to the heads of each of the 21 ministries, the council comprises ministers without portfolio and specially appointed advisors. Cabinet ministers serve a four-year term. The King can grant four-year extensions by Royal Decree.

The Council of Ministers carries out the active business of government. Only resolutions passed by a majority vote are binding. In the event of a tie, the King has the casting vote. The King must approve all Council decisions before they can be implemented. *See also* GOVERNMENT.

CURRENCY. Saudi Arabian paper currency, called the Saudi riyal, was introduced in 1952. The notes come in denominations of 1 (brown), 5 (purple), 10 (grey and purple), 50 (green), 100 (brown and green), 200 (brown and green), and 500 (blue and green). Coins, called *halalahs*, come in denominations of 5, 10, 25, and 50. One Saudi riyal equals 100 *halalahs*. The abbreviation, SR, is usually written in front of the number, i.e. SR500, or SR10.50.

Halalahs have never been particularly popular in Saudi Arabia. Many merchants round the riyal amount up or down in order to eliminate the need for change. In banks it can be difficult to receive in cash the exact amount of a cheque if there are *halalahs* involved.

There are no restrictions on taking money into or out of Saudi Arabia.

D

DAIRIES. The history of the Saudi dairy industry began as recently as late 1975/early 1976 with the pioneer companies of Masstock, Sanabel, Moushaiga, and Al-Bach.

The first consideration was the choice of a suitable location. Few places in the Kingdom could meet all the basic requirements of abundant water supply, relatively favourable climate, and proximity to the consumer. Al-Kharj, in Saudi Arabia's Najd region, became the favoured site.

In a desert, water is always a crucial concern. On a dairy farm the burden reaches a special magnitude. Each cow requires approximately 757 litres of water per day (this figure includes the watering of crops and the cleaning of the processing plants). Multiplied by many thousands of cows, not to mention requirements for crops and the cleaning of processing plants, the demands quickly become enormous.

Climate's role is equally indispensable. A combination of heat and humidity produces heat stress in the herds. Cows can withstand fairly high temperatures as long as the humidity remains low. However, even in the prevalent dryness of the Najd, the severe summers demand special protection and unique methods. Unlike cows in lusher settings, Saudi herds do not graze freely on open pastures. Barns or shade-covered paddocks shelter the animals and their daily feed supplies are brought directly to them.

Some methods of combatting heat not only make the cows more comfortable but increase production. 'Induced chill factor', for example, allows the animals to receive a constant spray of water while feeding from central troughs in their barns. Simultaneously, fans blow air onto the damp cows, thereby lowering their body temperatures. This heightens their appetites, making them eat more and thus produce more milk.

Cows feed at a central trough inside their barn in the Najd.

Less vital but certainly significant is the matter of locality for logistical purposes. From the central situation of the Najd, it takes distributors no longer than 40 hours to reach even the most remote area.

Last but certainly not least came the herds themselves. A government freight subsidy and other incentives substantially reduced the considerable start-up costs. A larger portion of the available funds could therefore be devoted to acquiring pedigree stock – a stipulation made by the Saudi government for anyone wishing to benefit from the generous financial assistance. Farms which began their herds with animals of correct genetic background have reaped the benefits. This investment in quality has provided excellent breeding stock and high milk yields.

After surviving numerous complications and setbacks, it came as an unexpected discovery to the dairies to learn that almost 90% of the population didn't want milk. Sales were encouragingly high but consumption of the milk in its natural form was minimal. Most consumers turned the milk into *laban*, a cultured, yoghurt-type drink. The dairies had not taken into consideration the fact that fresh cow's milk was alien to this nomadic society. Stomachs unaccustomed to cow's milk cannot easily digest it, so most people continued with their age-old diets of *laban*, using the milk base supplied by the dairies. Dairy scientists worked to discover how to produce *laban* in Saudi Arabia commercially. Even though a new generation of Saudis is growing up with fresh milk, *laban* still accounts for a substantial percentage of total liquid sales, although dairy advertising is eroding this statistic.

The responsibility of maintaining high standards of sanitation takes on an added dimension in Saudi Arabia where excessive outdoor temperatures favour the growth of unwanted bacteria. Also, because so much milk goes towards the production of *laban*, the most minute hint of antibiotics would interfere with the process. Dairies must therefore impose stringent controls and rigorous testing. As a result, the level of the general hygiene of milk is considerably higher in Saudi Arabia than it is in Europe or North America.

Producing enough milk to satisfy seasonal requirements developed into an unusual challenge. Sales in Saudi Arabia increase sharply during the hot weather and drop significantly during the cooler months. To coincide with this pattern, farmers had to make the cows abandon nature's plan of conceiving at the end of the summer, calving in November/December, and producing milk during the winter. Instead, Saudi cows calve in March and then conceive again in June/July, the hottest time of the year when they are under the greatest stress. This scientific manipulation ensures that the Kingdom has enough milk and *laban* to satisfy the copious summer demands.

In less than a generation, Saudi Arabia became a substantial producer of milk and its related products – no small achievement in a country where vegetation is sparse and cows were, until relatively recently, an unfamiliar species. Today, the largest dairy operation in the world is in Saudi Arabia.

D

DALLAH. This is the Arabic name given to the famous Saudi coffee pot, the symbol of Arabian hospitality. The pot has a distinctive pelican beak and a rounded lower half. Designs differ in various Middle Eastern countries; the traditional Saudi design is particularly plain. *See also* COFFEE RITUAL.

DAMMAM. This is the largest and longest settled city of the Dhahran-Dammam-Al-Khobar triangle. Its growth since the 1940s has been nothing short of spectacular. Once a minor fishing and pearling village, it is now the capital of the Eastern Province. *See also* EASTERN PROVINCE.

DAM. Arabia constantly combats a chronic shortage of water. In areas of heavy but seasonal rainfall, one of the most effective ways to ensure an ongoing supply of water has been the construction of dams. By storing water in times of excess and releasing it in times of need, dams prevent the erosion of valuable agricultural land, allow expanded cultivation, and eliminate the devastation caused by flash flooding.

The ancient but still imposing Samallaqi dam in Taif is one of the best preserved of the former dams. The ruins indicate that the builders used sophisticated building techniques and possessed a surprisingly advanced understanding of hydrology. Thanks to the effectiveness of Taif's skilfully built dams, productivity was increased to such an extent that the area became a prime agricultural and livestock producer.

The impressive Wadi Najran dam has had a major impact

on the area's water controls. The dam's catchment area is 4,800 square kilometres. The cylindrically arched dam wall can hold back 86 million cubic metres of water. At full capacity, the reservoir presents an area of approximately five square kilometres.

The Wadi Jizan dam stands out as the most impressive of the province's many projects. Heavy rains in the mountains used to cause devastating flash floods which claimed numerous lives, swept away communities and caused serious erosion. Now the torrents from five wadis are channelled into the dam's reservoir for selective release. The dam has proved so successful that the province plans eight similar projects.

DANCE. In public, traditional folk dances in Saudi Arabia are always performed by men. They vary from region to region. In the Eastern Province, the *allawaih* reflects the dangers and difficulties of the sea; the sword dance of the central Najd region, called the *ardha*, is the dance of warriors, as are the *al-majrour* and *al-sahbani.* The routines of desert life are portrayed in the *samire* dance. In the Western region, it is *al-mizmar* which is most popular.

Women, too, have their folk dances but these are performed at women-only events, such as weddings and other celebrations. Swinging their long, lustrous black hair to

***A group of Saudi men and boys perform the* ardha.**

the beat of the music, the women sensuously sway their bodies and move their hips. Like the men's dances, each region has its own style of women's dances.

DATE. In Saudi Arabia, late summer and early autumn are special times of the year. This is when the main harvesting of dates occurs. Despite the abundance and variety of local and imported foods, no Saudi household is without this nutritious fruit which has been a staple in the Middle East since remotest antiquity.

Medical science reinforces the folklore which boasts of the extraordinary nutritional and curative properties of the fruit and validates many of the old wives' tales and traditional treatments. The endorsements are impressive: oil extracted from date pits reduces the ill effects of heart disease; broth from stewed pits aids diabetics; eating the fruit eases pains in the joints and provides valuable nutrients to pregnant and nursing mothers. Scientists have found that dates possess a special hormone beneficial to women after delivery.

Fifteen dates daily satisfy the body's full alimentary requirements. The fruit's energy content is exceptionally high: one kilo of dates provides 3,000 units of energy compared with 800 units from a kilo of grapes. An old adage proclaims the date's versatility: *If you are hungry and eat dates, you will be full. If you are full and eat dates, it will be easy to digest.*

According to ancient documents, efforts to develop different strains and improve quality began more than 1,400 years ago. The poverty of many former communities and the constant high demand for dates kept the priority on inexpensive, low quality, high yield varieties. The primary requisites of affordability and abundancy restricted potential advances. Progressive technology and improved economic conditions of recent years have afforded widespread experimentation. Because so many other foods supplement today's diets, high yield is not as vital as it once was, although even this has improved due to better husbandry.

So far more than 400 commercial classifications of dates have been recorded in the Kingdom. Experts readily distinguish varieties by shape (oval or round, large or small), colour (reddish, or bright or dark yellow), and taste. Connoisseurs describe the taste and texture of a top-grade date as akin to truffle chocolates, whereas lesser grades have an almost tough consistency, rather like soft toffee in comparison.

In Saudi Arabia some of the most select varieties are *sukkary, khllass, sillej*, and *nbute sayf*. The lower grade *rzeiz* is commonly used in processing and is favoured for its high sugar content. The proportion of flesh to sugar, together with the taste, give dates their market value.

Dates develop in four stages. The first, *khalal*, produces green, bitter fruit. This ripens to *balah*, the red or yellow phase when the date is most nutritious, but for most tastes still too strong. At *rutab*, when the date is half brown and half yellow or red, the rough and smooth textures pleasantly combine to make this stage the most popular. Approximately 30 per cent of dates are eaten as *rutab. Rutab* also provides the highest profit margin. They can be stored in the freezer (not the refrigerator) and sold throughout the year, particularly at Ramadan. When the dates have fully ripened and turned completely brown they are called *tamr*. At this last stage they are considered 'cooked'.

As a result of liberal government incentives, Saudi Arabia now grows more dates than any other country in the world. Al-Ahsa grows more dates than all other areas combined. Hofuf, Al-Ahsa's main city, is the centre for bulk business and processing plants.

One million kilos of dates pass through Hofuf's bulk date market annually. The flurry of activity begins early in the morning when farmers arrive with their truckloads of traditional baskets, each holding 60 kilos of dates. Auctioneers noisily compete with each other to sell the dates in four-basket groupings called a *men*. Government officials maintain strict control. As the morning progresses, the mountains of dates rise higher. Workers steadily pack the fruit into 5- or 10-kilo bags or large tins in preparation for bulk sales throughout the country and abroad.

Date processing companies offer an important sales outlet. Farmers bring their dates to the factories in plastic crates which hold 20 kilos of fruit. These relatively small units make cleaning and processing more efficient. On arrival, the dates undergo a spot inspection to test for overall quality. Accepted deliveries immediately enter fumigation rooms for 24 hours to destroy possible insect life or bacteria.

The next stage involves a series of specialized cleaning procedures using desalinated water and superchlor. In Saudi Arabia, chemical additives are kept to a minimum (and often not used at all) so that colour, taste and texture remain unaffected.

After thorough cleansing, the dates are separated into three categories: top grade, medium grade, and for use as date paste. Dates which do not meet these standards are used as animal feed.

In the final step before packing and shipping, the dates enter a dehydration/hydration room or computerized tunnel where fan drying removes excess surface moisture. The dates will rot if the humidity level reaches 20 per cent

It takes only 1 1/2 days for a date to complete the entire cycle, from purchase to package. However, due to the low storage capacity in fumigation rooms, a large percentage of the dates goes to cold storage areas which maintain a constant temperature of -2ºC to -4ºC, allowing indefinite preservation.

DATE PALM. As one of the few trees which grew successfully in Arabia's arid conditions, the date palm (*Phoenix dactylifera*) was esteemed as a generous provider of many of early man's basic needs, including household items, building materials, fuel, fertilizers, and animal feed. Horticulturalists state that the tree has been cultivated for about 8,000 years.

Date palms grow as high as 30 metres. Each tree will have either male or female flowers. Fruit grows only on female trees. In commercial operations, the trees undergo artificial fertilisation. Date palms begin producing fruit at three to five years of age. The fruit grows in large bunches of as many as 1,000 dates. Each female tree bears between five and ten bunches. A tree reaches its full maturity at 12 years.

While modern advances have eroded the former indispensability of the date palm, its valuable contributions continue. Government intervention has revived the palm's prominence as a major source of income in the irrigable desert and scientific developments have found innovative methods of adapting the tree and its fruit to contemporary needs. *See also* DATE.

DEATH. Muslims receive the news of a death with the expression *Inna lillahi wa inna ilayhi rajiun* (we are from God and to God we shall return). The burial is followed by a three-day period of mourning.

A youngster climbs high in a date palm to pick ripe dates.

Outstanding debts and special bequests are paid from the deceased's estate before dividing the remainder among the heirs. Islamic law clearly defines all possible permutations of inheritance. *See also* BURIAL; MOURNING.

DESALINATION. Without the technology of water desalination, the Kingdom's tremendous growth in recent years would not have been possible. The treated waters of the Gulf and the Red Sea provide vital supplements to existing springs and groundwater.

Desalination plants were first introduced in the Kingdom in the 1920s, during the reign of King Abdul Aziz. Since that time, the number of plants has mushroomed to 27 in 2001. More than 2,000 kilometres of pipes transport treated water throughout the Kingdom. Some of the flow is stored in the 108 specially built reservoirs.

In only one generation, production has increased 100-fold. Desalination plants provide 70 per cent of the Kingdom's drinking water. This is currently 775 million cubic metres per day. Projects under construction will increase this to more than 3,028 million litres per day. Electricity generated by the stations yields 21 per cent of Saudi Arabia's supplies. The desalination facility at Jubail is the largest in the world.

DESERT. One of the first images conjured up by the words 'Saudi Arabia' is that of vast sand deserts. The legendary Nafud in the north of the country, the narrow arc of reddish sands called Al-Dahna south of the Nafud, and the Empty Quarter (Rub Al Khali) in the south certainly justify such a notion. But many thousands of kilometres of Saudi Arabia's terrain also comprise arid, stony plains and dramatic escarpments. The common denominator is that the regions are generally uncultivated and have sparse populations.

In terms of climate, the desert is a place of extremes. In the hottest months, temperatures often exceed 50ºC. The range between day and night temperatures can be more than 30 per cent. In winter, this drop can even result in frost. Rainfall is sporadic and does not necessarily fall in the same place each year, nor does it necessarily fall each year. The Empty Quarter, for example, might not witness rain for as much as ten years. Punishing sandstorms can suddenly appear and blow for days, making travel next to impossible.

Survival in the desert is a test of endurance. For the bedouin tribes who make this hostile environment their home, this means constant migration in search of vital water and grazing sources. For plants and animals it has meant adapting to a life of harsh winds and sun and little water. Yet, a moderate rainfall can make the desert come alive with vegetation that may have remained dormant for years. In an apparently barren landscape, the miracle of life is particularly dramatic. *See also* NAFUD; EMPTY QUARTER.

DESERT DIAMOND. In ancient times when the Arabian peninsula enjoyed a wetter climate, heavy rains washed pebbles of igneous and metamorphic rock and quartz, along with limestone, sand, and silt from the Hijaz mountains towards what is now the Arabian Gulf. In the process, desert diamonds were deposited in a great gravel basin known as Al-Dibdibah Plain. Al-Qaysumah, southeast of Hafr Al-Batin is the most famous place to hunt for desert diamonds, or Al-Qaysumah diamonds, as they are called locally. They can also be found in a narrow band that stretches from the outskirts of Riyadh to the Iraqi border.

The desert diamond begins life as a milky-coloured stone that is translucent when held to the light. They are most easily found on the hard, pebbly desert surfaces at dawn and before dusk, when the soft light reflects on the stones.

The quartz-based desert diamond is from the same family of macro-crystalline minerals as the amethyst, smoky topaz, and the citrine. On the Mohs scale, used for gauging the hardness of gems, desert diamonds have a hardness equal to that of a garnet, about 7-8, compared to cubic zircon at 5 and a carbon diamond at 10.

The size of the diamond is based on its carat weight. The desert diamond is heavier than the carbon diamond; therefore, when measured against a carbon diamond, the desert diamond is about 19 per cent smaller at the same carat weight.

Like carbon diamonds, desert diamonds can be cut in a variety of shapes and sizes but most people prefer the brilliant cut because it gives the gem the best possible sparkle.

When buying desert diamond jewellery, look for clear, brilliant stones that are well faceted. Do not accept stones that have imperfections, including cracks or discoloration.

Despite their growing popularity, desert diamonds are still remarkably affordable. Perhaps because it is so inexpensive and therefore not worth the time for commercial jewellers, jewellery made from desert diamonds is usually obtainable only from individual entrepreneurs. Many jewellers, particularly those outside the Kingdom, are unfamiliar with the stones and may insist that the gems are synthetic.

DESERT TRUFFLE. In classical Arabic, this fungus is known as *kema*. Colloquially, it is referred to as *fag'a*, meaning sprouter.

Rains in November and December bring a harvest of desert truffles beginning in late January or early February. It is said that the rains must be accompanied by lightning, as ozone is a necessary ingredient. If there are no end-of-year rains, there are no truffles.

Truffles can be found where there are patches of greenery in sandy areas of desert. A small rise in the sand gives the clue of the treasure beneath the surface. Gently using a knife to dig around the rise ensures the protection of a second truffle which may be growing underneath the more mature growth. By covering the second plant and waiting for a couple of weeks, a second 'harvest' is assured. It is interesting to note that truffles will never grow in compacted sand, for example in areas where cars have driven.

The first growth is small and not good to eat. By late February there is an abundance of the two popular varieties: the large, smooth, white *zubaidi* and the smaller, grooved, richer, black or brown *khlassi*. The *khlassi* must be carefully cleaned with a small brush in order to remove all the sand. A fourth growth remains in the ground and is eaten only by animals. Humans who eat this variety can suffer from diarrhoea.

Desert truffles are most commonly cooked with rice. The odorless fungus has a subtle, woody taste.

Some farms just outside Riyadh are now starting to grow truffles commercially.

DHAHRAN. The city of Dhahran forms part of the Dhahran-Dammam-Al-Khobar triangle. Dhahran grew up around the huge Aramco compound and the Aramco Exhibit, a popular museum illustrating the history of oil in Saudi Arabia. The University of Petroleum and Minerals is also based here. Dhahran used to be the site of an international airport but this now has been relocated 100 kilometres north of the old airport. *See also* EASTERN PROVINCE.

DHOW. The ancient tradition of boat building can still be found in the Gulf area. Craftsmen carve the beautiful teakwood boats without plans, relying solely on long experience and unerring eye. Traditionally, the teakwood planks of the *dhows* were sewn together with coir (rot-resistant coconut fibre rope) threaded through drilled holes. Modern *dhow* builders use nails, cotton sails have been replaced with spun or laminated polyester, and aluminium or carbon fibre fittings mingle with the elegant wood. In spite of these concessions, craftsmen continue to follow such time-tested routines as building the hull planking and then adding the framework. Much of the finishing work is done *in situ*.

The generic term *dhow* is an anglicized adaptation of the Persian *dawh* or the Swahili *daw*, meaning 'boat'. The *dhow* is distinctive for its square sterns and huge lateen sails which have been used in Arabian waters at least since 400 BC. These sails were originally triangular but, to improve sailing ability, a leading edge was formed by cutting off the forward angle, resulting in a four-sided sail that, nevertheless, looks triangular. The *dhow* is

A racing* dhow *catches the wind in its huge lateen sails.

unique in its ability to carry more sail in proportion to its size than any other sailing boat. Over the centuries, the design evolved, taking the most practical features from the merchant fleets of India, Malaysia, Portugal, Holland, and England.

Dhows vary in size from the small 25-ton coastal vessels to the 300-ton ocean-going *booms* which were used mainly for cargo. The *sambuq* was the Gulf's preeminent pearling vessel. Its design incorporates features from Indian and European boats. The square stern, for example, was influenced by Portuguese galleons. Its short keel made it ideal for the Gulf shallows and the necessary quick turns executed by the oarsmen.

Although other means of transportation have largely replaced the *dhow*, the silhouettes of these elegant craft can still be seen on both the Red Sea and the Gulf. Today they are almost always motorized. They are used primarily for fishing, as small cargo vessels, and as pleasure craft. They are also popular as racing boats in the Emirates.

DHUB. In Saudi Arabia, *dhub* lizards are found in sandy or stony arid and semi-arid desert areas. The most common species in the Kingdom is *Uromastyx aegyptia microlepis*.

Their mainly vegetarian diet, provided by shrubs, weeds, seeds, roots, and red and yellow flowers, is sometimes augmented by insects. Sharp jaw brims enable the animal to crack seed shells and chew hard roots. Adult spiny-tailed lizards hardly ever drink water; they rely on food sources for moisture and absorb humidity through their skin.

Dhubs live in burrows up to 10 metres long by two or three metres deep in the sand. Usually these exist in colonies, with burrows spaced about 20-50 metres apart. Snakes, scorpions, and small mammals often share *dhub* tunnels. Although *dhubs* usually wait until the temperature drops before exiting their burrows, they enjoy sunbathing. This causes their skin to change from sand/brown/grey to light grey, sometimes with yellow, beige, or black heads, or bright yellow all over. *Dhubs* hibernate during the winter months, from October to February.

Mating season begins in April/May. Males and females are notoriously selective about potential mates. The male performs circular dances beside or on top of the chosen partner who, despite his efforts, may reject him by flipping on her back. *Dhubs* begin reproducing when they are about four years old. They carry between 15-40 eggs for 42 days and then bury them in soft soil, checking on them periodically. Hatchlings emerge after 80-90 days and are immediately independent. They usually grow to a length of 60-80 centimetres but there have been sightings of 'giant' *dhubs* which exceed a metre.

The easy availability of meat in recent years has diminished the importance of the *dhub* as a protein supplement for the bedouin who call the reptile 'the fish of the desert': its cooked flavour is similar to that of fish without having a fishy smell. Traditionally, the lizard is slow-cooked with rice, similar to the preparation of *kapsa* (see *food*) but simmered for a longer period of time.

Now, city-dwellers hunt the large lizard for sport, an activity which has fast diminished the *dhub* population and put it on the endangered species list. Other predators include birds of prey, wolves, foxes, and wild dogs. With only its thrashing, spiny tail, its teeth, and its fast legs for defense, the *dhub* is not difficult to catch.

DIR'IYYAH. Along the banks of the Wadi Hanifa, nearly 20 kilometres north-west of Riyadh's city centre, lies the ancient oasis town of Dir'iyyah. The history of Dir'iyyah goes back to the middle of the 15th century. The land was originally owned by Ibn Dir, who gave the settlement its name in 1446. Three hundred years later, the former village had become one of the Arabian peninsula's major cities, an active commercial and cultural centre. In 1744, an historically important alliance was made between Muhammad Ibn Saud of Dir'iyyah and the renowned religious reformer Muhammad Abdul Wahhab. Abdul Wahhab promised Ibn Saud military support as long as he swore to rule according to the tenets of Islam.

In 1765 Muhammad Ibn Saud's son Abdul Aziz became the ruler. He immediately began to extend his authority eastward to the Al-Ahsa region and south towards Najran. By 1818 he had made his presence felt enough to alarm the Turks who sent an Egyptian army to recover their lost territory. It cost the Egyptians 10,000 men and a six-month siege but eventually they captured Dir'iyyah, destroying the town and cutting all the trees. The capital was transferred to Riyadh in 1824.

Dir'iyyah's outer wall was originally nearly seven kilometres long. The city itself consisted of several quarters, the most famous of which were Al-Turaif and Al-Bhairi. The former lay on a southwest hill which surveyed all quarters of the city. The Al-Saud palaces, administration offices, important residences and stables were situated in this area. The ruler's palace can be seen in the southeast of the quarter on the bank of the Wadi Hanifah. The Dar Al-Mal (state treasury) lay to the south. The great mosque, in the northern area, was a place for both worship and learning. In the middle of the quarter there existed a public Turkish bath, a reflection of the urban progress of the city.

Al-Buhairi quarter lay on the eastern bank of Wadi Hanifah, just opposite the Turaif quarter. In Al-Buhairi, Shaikh Muhammed ibn Abdul Wahhab had his home, mosque, and school. A busy market place thrived on the slope of the quarter facing the Wadi Hanifah.

Extensive restoration of Dir'iyyah has been underway for several years. When completed, the site will be a fine testament to an important part of the country's history.

DIVORCE. The tenets of Islam make divorce relatively straightforward. Islamic law does not require the parties to divulge the reason they seek a divorce. This eliminates the risk of perjury or family embarrassment. According to Muslim thinking, the public disclosure of unappeasable differences seldom motivates conciliation. On the contrary, it can estrange couples further. However, this does not mean that attempts are not made to settle disputes. Each party must appoint a mediator who tries to arrive at a mutually agreeable settlement. If these efforts fail, the divorce proceeds.

The phrase *I divorce you* dissolves a marriage. These words, not necessarily spoken in front of the spouse, must be reported to a *qadhi* (judge) in front of two witnesses in order for a formal document to be issued.

Despite its simplicity, the procedure is binding. The couple may remarry one another up to three times. After the third divorce, or if a spouse says *I divorce you thrice*, the parties cannot remarry each other until the wife has married and divorced someone else first. Because of the severity of the action, such a drastic step is not usually taken without due consideration.

A divorce is not only void but forbidden unless the man is

in a rational frame of mind and the woman is in a state of 'fresh purity'. This means it must be more than 40 days after childbirth or more than 10 days after her menstrual period. Nor can she have had intercourse after reaching this 'pure' state.

DJAMBIA. *See* JAMBIA.

DOORS. *See* ARCHITECTURE.

DOWRY. The dowry (*mahr*) is intended to provide for the bride's financial security. On a more symbolic level, *mahr* serves to compensate the girl and her family for their mutual 'loss'. The social standing of the bride and the relationship between her family and that of the groom determines the size of the *mahr*. Closely related families request only modest payments, while distant relations or unrelated families often demand considerably higher payments. In former times, dowries took the form of camels, clothes, or other valuables. Today, gold jewellery is the common commodity. Alternatively, cash in the region of SR50,000 is paid. Because the *mahr* can create an excessive burden on the groom and his family, the government encourages the adoption of a standard fee of SR40,000.

Before Islam, dowries were paid to the bride's relatives or guardians. The *Qur'an*, however, decrees that the groom must pay the dowry in a lump sum directly to the bride before the marriage. If the groom should die before the marriage, his executors must discharge this duty before all others from his estate.

Islamic law has no community of property, so the dowry and any post-marital acquisitions belong solely to the wife. She can use them in any way she sees fit, although she may voluntarily return all or part to her husband.

DRESS. Traditional Saudi dress has remained virtually

unchanged for hundreds of years. The Saudi unwillingness to depart from their distinctive garb is exemplified in their response to early 20th century Turkish occupation forces whose attempt to replace the *ghutra* and *agal* with the Turkish cap met with staunch resistance. Riots ensued and *Death is better than the Turkish cap* became a common rallying slogan.

The western regions of Saudi Arabia have distinctive clothing styles. In Asir, for example, both men and women wear a straw hat called a *tafashah* to protect them from the sun. Tassled headscarves for women are found only in Taif and Asir. *See also* ABAYA; BISHT; BURQA; FARWA; GHUTRAH; IGAAL; SIRWAAL; TAQIYAH; TARHA; THOBE; VEIL; WOMEN'S DRESS.

DUST DEVIL. These eddies of dust and sand blow in from the desert like mini tornadoes. They usually disappear quite quickly and are seldom strong enough to cause much damage. If they meet an open window or door in their path, however, the result is a significant deposit of fine dust.

E

EASTERN PROVINCE. This is the largest of Saudi Arabia's 14 governorates or administrative regions. Its borders extend as far north as Kuwait and Iraq and as far south as Qatar. The low-lying desert steppe in this part of the Kingdom is broken by escarpments, sandstone cliffs, and salt marshes. An ancient salt mine at Abqaiq is still in operation.

Archaeological evidence indicates that the coastal lands of the Eastern Province have been inhabited for thousands of years. Communities prospered as a result of pearling, fishing, and trade.

One of the many innovative sculptures which adorn the corniche in Dammam, Eastern Province.

In modern history, the region has gained renown as the home of Saudi Arabia's vast petroleum reserves. Directly or indirectly, life in the Eastern Province revolves around the flourishing oil industry.

E

The Kingdom's minority Shia (also called Shi'ite) Muslims have a large representation in the Eastern Province, particularly in the town of Qatif, one of the oldest settlements in the Kingdom. *See also* DHAHRAN; DAMMAM; AL KHOBAR; AL-AHSA; HOFUF; OIL.

EID AL-ADHA. This feast of sacrifice, or 'greater feast', signifies the end of the *hajj*. Animals are slaughtered in commemoration of Abraham's willingness to sacrifice his son. Much of the meat is distributed to the poor. As with *eid al-fitr*, Muslims offer special prayers, dress in new clothes, visit each other, and offer gifts, particularly to children. Business and government offices close during these festivities which last from four days to two weeks, depending on whether the organization is government or non-government.

EID AL-FITR. To serve as a transition from the strict abstinence of Ramadan to the normal routine of the rest of the year, Muslims celebrate with a period of festivity called *eid al-fitr*. This 'lesser feast' begins on the first day of the month of Shawwal and normally continues to the second or third day of Shawwal, though government offices and some businesses close for longer.

After communal prayers, usually at dawn, families and friends gather to feast. During the day they exchange visits and gifts. The celebration is marked by wearing new clothes and eating distinctive *eid* sweets. Just as Ramadan is a time of spiritual bonding, the *eid* reinforces social ties and encourages generosity. *See* HEJIRA.

ELEPHANT ROAD. In the year AD 571 the governor of Yemen led a team of war-trained elephants to Makkah with the audacious intention of removing the sacred *ka'ba* to Yemen. Despite their valiant efforts, the local population was unable to resist the onslaught. Then, according to tradition, just as the success of the plunderers seemed secure, Allah sent flocks of birds to bombard the elephants and warriors with stones. Only one of the attacking soldiers survived. He returned to Yemen to report on the army's failure and to bring the stern warning to his government never to repeat such blasphemy. Traces of the road can still be found in western Arabia.

EMPTY QUARTER. The infamous 650,000 square kilometre Empty Quarter or Rub Al-Khali has the well-deserved reputation of being one of the most desolate places on earth. Even the hardy bedouin find most of this extensive stretch of sand desert inhospitable and uninhabitable. Nevertheless, this impressive wasteland has attracted great travellers. In 1930 Bertram Thomas became the first European to make a successful crossing. In later years, he was followed by St. John Philby and Wilfred Thesiger. Each of them wrote a memorable account of his adventures.

Rainfall in the beautiful but treacherous area is light and sporadic, seldom falling in the same place in consecutive years. Many parts receive no rain for periods of as much as ten years. Summer temperatures frequently soar above 50°C. On winter nights it can drop to below freezing.

Spectacular shifting sand dunes in the Empty Quarter, sculptured by the winds, come in many shapes and sizes. They are often like small mountains, averaging 200 metres tall and rising to more than 300 metres. Iron oxide gives the sand its reddish colour.

F

F

FALCONRY. Falconry had its beginnings in prehistoric times and remains a virtually unchanged method of hunting. It was introduced from Arabia into Europe by the Crusaders and the Arabs who invaded Spain. Problems of decreasing hunting grounds, prey, and falcons caused a decline in the sport but, thanks to better conservation and improved breeding techniques, there has been a significant international revival.

In the language of falconers, only the larger, female hawk is referred to as a falcon. The male is the tiercel. Birds taken from the nest before they learn to fly are called eyas. Wild-caught immature birds are passagers, while adults are called haggards.

In Arabia, hawks are valued for their ability to pursue quarry which far exceeds them in size. Gazelle and the turkey-like houbara bustard are favourite prey.

A hooded falcon awaits the falconer's command.

Arabia's open spaces are ideal for these long-winged birds whose spectacular hunting methods include soaring and stooping from great heights at speeds of almost 322 kilometres per hour.

Because the heat of Arabia does not allow the birds to moult normally, new birds are obtained each season. Their training is therefore briefer and more intense than procedures used in other parts of the world. Good hawkers can train a year-old hawk in 13 days; it takes up to 25 days for a 2- to 3-year-old hawk. Because this requires frequent contact with the birds, it is not unusual to see trainers carrying hooded falcons everywhere on their gloved fists.

The successful training of a bird requires immense patience and a profound understanding of the bird's psychology. The challenge of turning a wild creature into an ally, if not a friend, is cause for much pride and satisfaction in those whose skills are rewarded.

FAMILY. The Saudi considers his family all-important and deserving of the greatest loyalty. 'Family' in the Arab sense extends beyond the immediate relatives to include even the most remote members of a common tribe. A Saudi does not see himself as an individual as much as part of a whole: the family and, to a lesser extent, the tribe. His responsibilities are to the group rather than to himself.

The entire culture is based on kinship, so roots are all important. Saudis are ultimately judged by their backgrounds and not by financial status. A family's history of such intangibles as generosity, courage, and honour are far more meaningful than the current success or failure of individual members, although this, too, will be woven into the tribe's reputation. Family ties are ingrained from an early age and take precedence over any other obligations or relationships.

An Arab proverb proclaims, *My brother and I against our cousin; my cousin and I against the stranger.*

Many Saudis, particularly in rural areas, continue the tradition of the extended family, where it is not uncommon for three generations to live together under the same roof. Depending on the size of the house, unmarried children and married sons with their wives and children may live with the parents, at least until the sons become established and start their own homes. In the cities, where greater employment opportunities offer increased possibilities of financial independence, there is a growing trend towards smaller, nuclear families.

The oldest male is the head of the family or tribal unit but a father of a sub-family heads his own household. He is responsible for its economic and social well-being, although he relies on support and advice from family members beyond his jurisdiction. The eldest son is the second most important person in a family. He is entrusted with everything, usually to the exclusion of his siblings.

In domestic matters, women rule, with the eldest female having the greatest influence. Mothers are accorded special respect, as reflected in the Arabic saying, *The way to paradise is through obedience to mothers.*

Saudi families tend to be large. In conversation, Saudis frequently refer to 'cousins'. There can be so many 'cousins' that foreigners sometimes assume it is a catch-all word used as a substitute for 'brother', 'uncle', or 'friend'. Usually, however, the terminology is perfectly apt. Large families produce numerous cousins!

FARASAN ISLANDS. The Farasans are a grouping of coral islands in the Red Sea off the coast of Saudi Arabia's southwestern province of Jizan. The largest of the group,

Farasan Al-Kabir, covers an area of 395 square kilometres. Most of the 20 large islands and more than 100 islets are unpopulated.

The Farasans are a popular destination for scuba divers and nature lovers. Jacques Cousteau, the famous underwater explorer, said of the Farasans, *To learn about the Farasan's reef structures and marine biological richness would take a lifetime.*

The unspoiled islands have a wealth of bird life; pelicans and flamingoes fish and nest undisturbed. Rare turtles lay their eggs on the quiet beaches of the remote islands. The reefs in the vicinity of the archipelago are particularly spectacular. They sustain and shelter an exotic variety of marine creatures. Coral and shellfish fossils on the islands are plentiful.

Although excavations have not been extensive, the islands have rich archaeological potential. So far, three important pre-Islamic settlements and a number of lesser sites have been discovered.

Local islanders traditionally earned their living by fishing. Village cooperatives protected areas from over-fishing. The recent introduction of factory fishing has interfered with this delicate balance. Efforts are now being made to zone the Farasans for the exclusive use of local fishermen so that this unique resource can be preserved.

Since there is no airport on the islands, access is by car ferry from Jizan. The trip takes approximately four hours. Alternatively, private boats can be chartered.

FARWA. In particularly cold weather, many Saudis wear a *farwa*. The original design of the *farwa* consisted of a single sheepskin. It has now evolved into a long, sleeved wool or canvas coat lined with several sheepskins (or synthetic fibres). Like the lighter weight *bisht* or *mishlah*, the *farwa* has no buttons or zippers. A simple geometric pattern often decorates the upper middle back area. The *farwa* is such an effective deterrent against the cold that the bedouin often use it as bedding during the winter.

FAUNA. Despite the fact that so much of Saudi Arabia appears to be uninhabitable, and the fact that indiscriminate hunting has driven many birds and animals to the verge of extinction, wildlife exists in interesting diversity.

The most commonly seen creatures are camels, desert dogs, horses, gekkos, camel spiders, sheep, goats, and baboons (in the mountain regions), not to mention the rich selection of fish from the Red Sea and the Gulf. Much of the remainder of Saudi Arabia's fauna are either nocturnal and/or make their habitats in remote desert or mountain regions.

Members of the dog family *Canidae* (jackals, foxes, and wolves) and the cat family *Felidae* (Arabian leopard, cheetah, caracal lynx, and sand cat) are well represented.

The wildlife found in Arabia has had to adapt to the peninsula's harsh climatic and geographic conditions. Their feet, for example, are often padded and broad in order to traverse the hot sand; ears may be large in order to hear for great distances, beige and brown colourings help the animals to blend in with their surroundings and, perhaps most important, many of the species have learned to go for long periods with little water.

Many of the Kingdom's mammals, such as the baboon (*Papio hamadryas*), the white-tailed mongoose (*Ichneumia albicauda*), and the hyrax (*Procavia capensis*) are African in origin. These migrants from long-ago ages before Arabia separated from the African land mass are found mainly in the higher elevations that stretch from Taif south to northern Yemen. The mountains and escarpments have a kinder climate and sufficient vegetation to hide and shelter the zoological population and feed its non-carnivorous members.

Reptiles abound, from poisonous and non-poisonous snakes, including cobras and deadly and aggressive vipers, to a wide variety of large and small lizards.

Uninhabited beaches bordering the Red Sea and the Gulf provide breeding grounds for several species of sea turtles. The governments of Gulf countries now protect these endangered amphibians.

More than 500 species of birds have been recorded in the region. Most of these are migratory, such as geese, ducks, kingfishers, swallows, and quail. Falcons are particularly prized. It takes only a short time to train them for hunting. The stone curlew (*Burhinus oedicnemus*) and the hoopoe lark (*Alaemon alaudipes*) are desert birds that are often sighted far from water. The southwest, with its high mountains and coastal areas, has the greatest variety of birdlife. The Raydah escarpment in the Asir has extensive juniper tree coverage that is ideal for birds. Only in this reserve are all the endemic species of Arabia found.

In 1986 King Fahd bin Abdul Aziz founded the National Commission for Wildlife Conservation and Development. Through a wide range of research and education programmes the NCWCD has made great strides in rescuing many indigenous species from the brink of extinction and in providing protection to those at risk. So far it has concentrated its captive-breeding efforts on oryx, houbara, ibex, and gazelles. *See also* ARABIAN HORSE; BABOON; CAMEL; CAMEL SPIDER; DHUB; FALCONRY; GAZELLE; GEKKO; HAMOUR; HOUBARA; IBEX; ORYX; SALUKI; SHEEP.

FIVE PILLARS OF ISLAM. A Muslim has five religious obligations, or *arkan* (pillars):

Shahada: The first pillar is *shahada*, or profession of faith: *Ashhadu an la ilaha illa-ilah; ashhadu an Muhammad al-rusool allah* (I bear witness that there is no god but God; I bear witness that Muhammad is God's messenger). The recital of the *shahada* in full as an act of unquestioning and fervent belief is the sole requirement for conversion to Islam. The statement must be made aloud, understanding its significance, at least once in every Muslim's life.

Salaat: Prayers (*salaat*) performed in a prescribed manner comprise the second pillar of faith and are a foremost condition of Islam. Individually or in groups, in public or in private, Muslims ritually wash themselves, face in the direction of the *ka'ba* in Makkah and pray five times daily: one-and-a-half hours before sunrise (*fajr*), midday (*dhuhr*), mid-afternoon (*asr*), sunset (*maghrib*), and nightfall (*isha*). In Saudi Arabia, all retail outlets are required to close for 20-30 minutes at each prayer time. Many businesses do not answer the telephone during prayer.

Zakaat. On a secular level, Islam requires its followers to care for the less fortunate. A compulsory philanthropy called *zakaat* (almsgiving) is imposed on all Muslims. This duty is met through the payment of an annual religious tax at both the corporate and individual levels. *Zakaat* contributes to social stability and ensures that the needs of the community are not neglected.

Sawm: As the fourth pillar, fasting (*sawm*) is an act of worship. It not only serves as exacting self-discipline but teaches through experience the deprivations of thirst and hunger.

The daylight hours of Ramadan, the ninth month of the *hejira* calendar, are entirely devoted to this regimen.

Exemptions are granted to pregnant, nursing, or menstruating women, the old or infirm, young children, the insane, and people travelling further than 80 kilometres. Anyone who breaks the fast must make up the days before the next Ramadan. Alternatively, they can feed one poor person for each fasting day missed.

Despite the difficulties of fasting, Muslims are expected to maintain their normal routines. Those who use Ramadan as an excuse to shirk work and other responsibilities effectively break their fast. Muslims must also refrain from losing control of their temper and their speech.

Traditionally, the fast is broken after the sunset prayer with a light snack, often fresh dates and water. A more substantial meal is taken after the fifth prayer (*isha*), usually about one and a half hours after dusk.

Hajj: Every Muslim shares the common religious goal of making the pilgrimage (*hajj*) to Makkah, the birthplace of the Prophet Muhammad and where he first received God's revelations. This fifth pillar of faith stipulates that the journey need only be made once in a lifetime and only if the pilgrim (*hajji*) is physically and financially able. *Hajj* cleanses pilgrims of sin; one prayer said in the Grand Mosque is equivalent to 100,000 prayers said elsewhere.

Islam preaches equality but perhaps nowhere is this more evident than during the pilgrimage. All pilgrims, regardless of social position, enter Makkah wearing a simple white seamless garment (*ihram*). Together, bound by their faith, they mingle to perform prescribed rituals of worship. Departure from the recognized pattern invalidates the pilgrimage. *See also* HAJJ; ISLAM; MAKKAH; MADINAH; QUR'AN; RAMADAN

FLAG. Saudi Arabia's distinctive green flag has been in existence since 1938. The Arabic text *There is no God but*

Allah, and Muhammad is His messenger is written above a single horizontal sword. It is the only flag where an inscription is the main design feature. The flag does not fly at half mast during periods of mourning.

FLORA. Despite the arid terrain of much of Saudi Arabia, few areas are permanently without vegetation. The most miraculous displays appear in the desert after the winter rains. In years of good rain, large areas of desert transform into vast tracts of greenery speckled with a wild array of flowers. Some are delicate, pastel varieties such as the desert camomile or the *al-khozama*; other are tall and boldly painted like the aloes.

Seeds or bulbs (corms) may lie dormant for as long as 20 years, waiting for the right conditions. When they finally sprout, the growth and dropping of seeds occur fleetingly. Those plants that stay in bloom for longer periods or which bloom annually despite the fact that there may have been little or no rain the previous winter are adept at extracting maximum moisture from minimum supplies. They tend to have lengthy tap roots that reach the deep groundwater as well as a system of feeder roots widely spread under the soil or sand surface. The extensive root network of some bushes, such as the sandwormwood (*Artemisia monosperma*), also helps to stabilize the movements of sand dunes.

Small leaf size, as displayed by the thorny acacia, reduces water loss through evaporation. Succulents, such as the purple daisy-like flowered *Delosperma abyssinica* or the cactus-like *Caralluma retrospiecens,* retain water in their fleshy leaves. Some trees and shrubs, such as the euphorbia or spurge (*Cactiform euphorbias*) or the adenium or desert rose (*Adenium arabicum*) store water in their stems and trunks.

Another mechanism to ensure survival of a species is staggered germination: only one seed at a time in a seed casing germinates. If there is not enough water to support the growth of the plant, the other seeds remain dormant until conditions improve.

While some seeds may be spiny and some plants toxic to discourage animal foraging, other plants have sweet scents or bright colours to attract birds and insects and thus ensure pollination.

Different areas of Saudi Arabia support different types of vegetation. Herbaceous flowering plants are common in the mountain regions. These include geraniums, asphodels, bladder dock, wild iris, heliotrope, scarlet pimpernel, and the aromatic purple lavender. Wadis often have growths of acacia woodlands. Asir's unique Raydah escarpment is famous for its lush juniper forest where some of the trees grow as high as 20 metres. At lower altitudes, trees such as olive, acacia, and pistachio trees grow in profusion.

Mangrove swamps thrive in the lagoons of the Farasan

Islands and in some of the coastal areas of the Red Sea and the Gulf. These flowering trees provide protection and important nutrients to juvenile fish and shrimp and help to prevent erosion. *Limonium* (sea lavender), *Salsola,* and *Suaeda* bushes tolerate the salty coastal conditions equally well.

F

The central Najd area has grass and steppe vegetation. Flowering perennials include daisies (*Scorzoneramusilii*), germanders (*Teucrium rigidum*), and the furry globe thistle (*Echinops spinosa*). Crisp fleabane (*Pulicaria crispa*), salt bushes, and *Rhanterium eppaposum* provide vital nourishment for foraging camels and sheep. All oases support large growths of date palms (*Phoenix dactyliftera*), a tree which needs dry, sunny weather when it is time for the fruit to ripen. *See also* DATE PALMS; TAMARISK.

FOOD. Thousands of years of interaction with many cultures as a result of trade routes and pilgrimage has inevitably influenced Saudi cuisine. What has emerged is a delightful marriage of flavours reminiscent of many nations but with a distinctly Saudi twist.

Dates have always formed an important staple of the Saudi diet. The Prophet Muhammad said, *The people of a house where there are no dates are hungry.* This fruit of the desert continues to play a prominent culinary role. Muslims break their fast during Ramadan with dates. Served with cardamom coffee, dates have come to symbolise the hospitality for which Saudi Arabia is so famous. A favourite Najdi winter dish is *hanaini*: dates mixed with coarse-milled brown wheat and clarified butter and sprinkled with black pepper. When dates are packed and left to sit, a thick, sweet syrup (*dibs*) forms. This by-product is added as a flavouring to other foods. *Muhammar*, for example, is a sweetened rice dish cooked in *dibs*.

Rice is another dietary staple. Saudi Arabia's per capita consumption averages 33 kilos each year. This equates to a need for more than 700,000 tons annually. Although rice is imported from all over the world, the preferred variety is Indian basmati, a long-grain rice with a faint fragrance. Many Saudi dishes, such as the famous *kapsa* (rice with lamb, either whole or in large chunks) require the accompaniment of vast quantities of rice. Saudis serve rice plain or with vegetables and spices and even rose water. The recipe for rice flavoured with tomatoes, nuts, and raisins, arrived centuries ago with pilgrims from Bukhara. It became known as *ruz Bukhari* and remains a firm favourite in the Hijaz.

Mutton, goat, and camel, cooked either on a bed of rice or stuffed with delicious blends of rice, nuts, herbs and spices, are the traditional meats of Arabia. In less affluent times, meat was eaten only on special occasions: for religious or social celebrations or to honour an important guest. Now most Saudis eat meat or poultry daily. *Kibbeh* (small oval mixtures of ground lamb and spices), *sambousek* (semi-circles or triangles of pastry filled with ground lamb, onions, and spices), and *shawarmas* (a cone of Arab bread filled with spit-grilled chicken or lamb and salad) are the equivalent of fast foods and an important feature of the Arab diet. With the exception of pork, which is forbidden by Islam, everything from ostrich to veal is readily available.

Coastal areas emphasise fresh seafood in their diets. The Gulf and the Red Sea teem with a rich variety of fish and shellfish, including grouper, red snapper, crab, and shrimp. *Samakh harrah*, fish coated with sesame seed paste (*tahini*) and *maglubat samak*, fish with rice, nuts, and spices, are two of the many local specialities. A perennial favourite, however, is fish simply fried and accompanied by rice and a salad.

Eastern Province food tends to be more piquant than

dishes in other parts of the country. This is a result of centuries of trading with the famous spice centres of the east. Each family has its own special blends of spices which they apply liberally to cooking.

F

Vegetarian dishes, too, have their place in Saudi cuisine. *Jareesh* is the hearty and nourishing outcome of blending cracked whole wheat, yoghurt, and clarified butter into a creamy, porridge-like consistency. *Hommos* (a purėed mix of chickpeas, *tahini*, lemon, and garlic), *baba ghanouj* (purėed baked eggplant, *tahini*, lemon, and garlic), and *tabouleh* (cracked wheat, chopped parsley, mint, tomato, and onion) are Mediterranean imports which have become fixtures in the Saudi diet. *Foul mudammas*, an Egyptian dish consisting of fava beans stewed in special pots with tomatoes and flavourings, is served at breakfast and dinner in Hijazi homes.

No matter whether a meal is meat, fish, or vegetable, bread is always an accompaniment. Even if the dish is bread-based, such as *marquq* (dough cooked with meat and vegetables) or *tharid* (similar to *marquq* but saturated with broth) there are plenty of fresh rounds of Arab bread. This not only served as an inexpensive filler in times of food shortages but also as a practical way to scoop up the hot food before cutlery came into common use.

Besides the ubiquitous coffee and tea, camel milk, *laban* (a liquid yoghurt), and fruit juices were the standard fare before the incursion of soft drinks. Because alcohol is forbidden, a refreshing mix of apple juice and sparkling water garnished with fresh mint and fruit pieces, known as Saudi 'champagne', is always on restaurant menus.

Meals traditionally ended with a presentation of fresh fruit, sometimes as a salad but usually still in the skin. Now the highly sweetened treats from other Arab countries are part of the Saudi regimen. Delicacies such as *kneifah, baklawa, nammurah,* and *katayef* have in common a pastry base flavoured with sugar, honey, lemon and nuts, often pistachios. Less sweet is the milky pudding *muhallabiyah.* No menu would be complete without *Om Ali*, a type of bread pudding which originated in Egypt, or *crème caramel*, from France via Lebanon.

Although many families now opt for the Western style of tables and chairs, traditional settings where numerous plates of food are placed on a *sufra*, a circular mat used as a table cloth or on a rectangular plastic cover on the floor can still be found, particularly in rural areas. Family and friends sit cross-legged around the perimeter of the display and use their right hands to serve themselves.

Islam forbids the eating of any derivatives from the pig, including gelatine. According to the strictest interpretation of the *Qur'an*, the one followed in Saudi Arabia, alcohol in any form is also forbidden. This means that such flavourings as pure vanilla extract should not be used despite the fact that the alcohol evaporates during cooking.

Despite the incursion of western-style fastfood outlets in recent years, traditional Saudi cooking predominates at celebrations and during Ramadan. Even those who opt for convenience on a day-to-day basis, take time to prepare the often labour-intensive recipes handed down by their mothers and grandmothers on special occasions.

Until recently, foreigners seldom experienced authentic Saudi cuisine unless they had the rare opportunity to visit a Saudi home or attend a wedding. Now, thanks to increasingly popular Saudi-themed restaurants, this culinary heritage is being shared with and appreciated by many. *See also* ARAB BREAD; CAMEL MEAT; COFFEE; DATES; DESERT TRUFFLES; HONEY; LABAN; RAMADAN FOOD; SHAWARMA; SPICE.

F

FOSSILS. The deserts of Arabia are a rich repository of clues to past life on earth. Specimens of land and sea creatures, both extinct and surviving, offer an interesting education. Fish and coral fossils, for example, tell us that parts of central Arabia were once covered in water. The remains of plants and animals reveal that the land areas of the region were lush enough to support a great variety of life forms.

In the Al-Dabtiyah area of the Eastern Province, palaeontologists have discovered bones from creatures as diverse as the Asian mastodon and the African crocodile.

FRANKINCENSE. *See* INCENSE.

FRANKINCENSE ROUTE. Today we romantically refer to the ancient trails from Oman across Yemen and up the length of western Arabia as the frankincense route. For countless generations, this trade lane reigned as one of the foremost in antiquity, witnessing the passage of some of the greatest riches of the known world. Ships from India and East Africa landed in the ports of Cana and Aden and joined land transports from southern Arabian cities heading northward. With equal regularity, caravans from Persia-Mesopotamia, Syria, Egypt, Greece, and Rome passed through the territories of western Arabia on their way to southern destinations.

The caravans originally travelled on well-constructed, paved highways. Still, the journey cannot have been easy. Coastal areas held the risk of malaria and the discomfort of high, humid temperatures. The endless stretches of mountain terrain proved both difficult and dangerous, not only in the geographical sense but also because of periodic tribal warfare, not to mention problems of provisioning for such large numbers of people and animals.

All along the route, cities and civilizations flourished.

The cities became not only the scenes of major mercantile activity but also prominent centres of culture as a result of the many learned travellers passing through. Western and southern Arabia wielded immense power in their control of the caravan routes. Most Arabian governments established seats convenient to the main trade lanes rather than in essentially agricultural districts, underlining the importance attached to commerce.

The present-day name of this famous route originates from the precious gum-resin, frankincense, which had already established itself as a valuable commodity more than 4,000 years ago. Demand for the product peaked in 200 BC. Historical references show that it had many applications in ancient life: it was used in religious ceremonies, for a variety of cosmetic functions, including that as a fixative in perfumes, and for a wide range of medicinal purposes. Pliny the Elder mentioned frankincense as an antidote to hemlock poisoning. Modern medicine has made studies of the gum-resin but, as yet, has found little scientific basis to validate the traditional cures. Today, frankincense is sought primarily as an incense.

Of course, the route did not only rely on frankincense for its success. The caravans carried a selection of aromatics, including the delicately scented rose attar and sandalwood. Myrrh, another gum-resin even more expensive than frankincense, was also popular. Jewels, silks, spices, and gold were some of the other luxuries that passed to and fro.

The business of spices and incense provided prodigious yearly incomes to regional rulers, including the fabled King Solomon, and made fortunes for the merchant class. As Strabo (*c.*64 BC-AD 23), the Greek historian and geographer noted, even a camel driver *might attain to some sort of wealth* as a result of the lucrative trade. Despite their nomadic and simple lifestyle, the bedouin, too, were attracted to the potential of easy money. They benefited by providing the camels necessary for the transport of the goods.

The entrepreneurial Nabataeans, an ancient civilization from northern Arabia, eventually abandoned the trading aspect of business in preference for the service side. In exchange for protection and vital water supplies, the Nabataeans levied a tariff of 25 per cent of the value of all the goods entering their territory. Because the strategic position of the Nabataean domain of Al-Hijr (now called Madain Saleh), the itinerant traders had no choice but to comply. The excessive financial burden imposed by the greed of the Nabataeans encouraged and even hastened major markets to seek cheaper, faster routes. The opening of the strait of Bab el-Mandeb at the southern tip of Arabia allowed direct sea traffic from Egypt to India. As a result, by AD 100, the importance of the ancient overland routes had dwindled and finally disappeared.

Arabia's frankincense route is probably one of the best known of the ancient trade lanes. For more than 2,000 years this well-travelled road witnessed the passage of some of the greatest riches of the known world. Denying any sense of loyalty, the road carried both invading troops and defending tribes; its presence helped small villages flourish into prosperous towns. *See also* INCENSE.

G

GAZELLE. The three types of gazelle common to Saudi Arabia are the *idmi* or mountain gazelle (*Gazella gazella*) and the *afri* or dorcas gazelle (*Gazella dorcas*), both of which are found mostly in the higher altitudes of the west and south-west, and the *rheem* or goitred gazelle (*Gazella subgutturosa*), which inhabits the gravel plains and sandy deserts of the central region. The *rheem* gets its name from a goiter-like swelling in the throat which males display throughout the mating season. Males rub the inky black excretion from the swelling onto plants and rocks to mark their territories.

Arabia's gazelles share similar colouring: white bellies, rump, and inner legs topped by a reddish brown coat over the rest of the body. A dark nose spot and flank stripe distinguish the *idmi*. *Afri* have a white face stripe and vague flank stripe, while the *rheem's* facial colouration is ill defined and it has no flank stripe. The dainty *afri* contrasts sharply with the stocky *rheem*. Perhaps because of its heavy build, the *rheem* is the only one of the three which does not 'stott'. This is the graceful ability to spring up, removing all four feet off the ground at the same time while keeping the legs stiff. This bouncing movement is used during play and at the approach of danger. Gazelles can gallop as fast as 70 kilometres/hour over short distances.

Horn shapes and lengths vary slightly: in the male *idmi*, the ringed, fairly straight horns which gently curve back and then forward (like an 's') measure 150-270mm; the *rheem* has straight, lyrate horns from 200-300mm; and the long-eared *afri* has straight, long horns which average 260-300mm. The horns of the female *afri* are shorter and more slender.

Herds rarely comprise adult males and females. Usually there are bachelor herds, territorial males, and herds composed of adult females and their immature offspring. Groups number 5-10 for the *idmi* and *afri* and 10-50 for the *rheem*. Male *rheem* gazelle defend their territory far more aggressively than the *idmi* or *afri*.

A rheem *gazelle.*

Gestation periods vary among the species: approximately 156 days for the *rheem*, 172 days for the *afri*, and 180 days for the *idmi*. Although gazelle generally reproduce in the spring when forage is most plentiful, birthing is not restricted to one season, as indicated by *idmi* females who have been known to give birth in September as well as March. *Idmi* tend to conceive in October; *rheem* are slightly later, mating November/December. Lambs suckle until the fourth or fifth month but can survive without milk after six weeks.

The King Khalid Wildlife Research Centre was founded in 1986 to manage the remaining herds of gazelle and eradicate the threat of tuberculosis. Kept in extensive preserves, their numbers have increased substantially.

GEKKO. This harmless little lizard (*Gekkonidae*) is a familiar sight on the walls and ceilings of buildings or sunning itself on warm rocks. Even when they can't be seen, the clicking noises they use to communicate with each other signal their presence. At night gekkos like to stay near lights so they can catch mosquitos, flies, and other insects, including cockroaches. With such an appetite for household pests, gekkos are definately good to have around.

Although there are several varieties of gekkos in Saudi Arabia, those found in homes and gardens most commonly have smooth, sand-coloured bodies (as opposed to ridged skin with more pigmentation). Their little feet have five widely-spaced 'fingers' with ball-shaped ends that can attach to virtually any surface.

If caught by a predator, a gekko has the unique capability of 'detaching' its tail. The appendage continues to twist and turn for awhile, hopefully distracting the predator while the gekko makes its escape.

GEOGRAPHY. Saudi Arabia covers 2,331,000 square kilometres of the Arabian peninsula. It shares borders with Jordan, Iraq, and Kuwait on the northern frontier, Qatar and the United Arab Emirates on the southeast, and Oman and Yemen to the south. The spectacular and varied landscape includes stony plains, sweeping sand deserts, salt marshes, escarpments, mountains, and fertile plateaus and oases.

The Kingdom has no permanent bodies of water, although sudden, heavy rainfalls can cause the *wadis* (dry river beds) to fill with alarming speed. The flow soon evaporates or soaks into the parched ground but the paradox of people drowning in the desert is not unheard of.

Grass and scrub vegetation cover the upland plateau of northern Arabia. Nomadic and semi-nomadic tribes use this area extensively to graze their herds. Wadi Al-Sirhan, a 300-metre-wide basin carved out of the surrounding plain, is evidence of an ancient inland sea.

A spine of rugged mountains, low in the north and increasingly higher in the south, separates the narrow Tihama coast on the west from the rest of the country. The highest peak, Al-Sooda, in the southwestern province of Asir, rises 2,700 metres above sea level.

Sloping eastward off the western range is the large central plateau commonly called the Najd. The western portion of the plateau is as high as 1,520 metres. This region consists mostly of sand and gravel deserts punctuated by isolated mountains and lush, spring-fed oases, many of which are located within the arc of the Tuwaiq escarpment. Extensive irrigation has increased the areas of cultivated land. Nevertheless, only about 2 per cent of the land is under cultivation. The Najd continues its gentle slope, giving way to sandy plains, marshes, and salt flats just before it reaches the irregular coastline of the Arabian Gulf.

Two of the earth's most formidable deserts, the Nafud in the north and the Empty Quarter (Rub Al-Khali) in the south, blanket much of Saudi Arabia. For the most part, these barren, inhospitable regions remain uninhabited except for nomadic tribes. *See* also ASIR NATIONAL PARK.

GEOLOGY. Geologically, the Arabian peninsula is divided into two sections: the Arabian Shield which forms the western third and the low-lying Arabian Shelf. It is believed that Arabia was once part of Africa. A massive split millions of years ago resulted in the Great Rift Valley which extends from East Africa through western Yemen and Saudi Arabia as far north as Jordan. During this upheaval, eastern Arabia tilted downward and formed the Arabian Gulf. The mountain range in what is now the Hijaz and Asir, originated as a chain of volcanoes and volcanic islands. The continental shift elevated these formations to heights that are believed to have been one of the largest ever to have existed. The impressive remains are only the roots of what once was.

The oldest formations of igneous and metamorphic rock, from the Precambrian period, contain minerals such as gold, silver, copper, zinc, iron, and magnesium. The younger layer of sedimentary rock, referred to as the Phanerozoic Cover, has deposits of bauxite, phosphate, clay, limestone, silica sand and lightweight aggregate. The compression over the eons of millions of tons of organic matter created the Kingdom's most important natural resources: oil and natural gas. Its known reserves represent 26 per cent of the world's supply.

The government is currently exploiting vast reserves of phosphate in the north of the Kingdom. Full production of the deposits would make Saudi Arabia the world's third largest producer of the mineral. After processing, magnesite deposits yield approximately 20,000 tons of high-grade, high-value electrofused magnesia annually. With the mining of these ores and its substantial deposits of gold, silver, copper, bauxite and other minerals, Saudi Arabia hopes to reduce its financial dependency on oil. *See also* DESERT; OIL.

GHUTRA. This white head covering is worn by Saudi men. It serves as both a protection from the sun and as a convenient nose and mouth cover in sand storms. The large square of cotton or cotton blend is folded diagonally and placed on top of the *taqiyah* (skull cap). Most men leave the *ghutra* or *shama'agh* on at all times, except when relaxing at home. It is impolite to ask a Saudi to remove his head covering. *See also* SHAMA'AGH.

GOLD. *See* JEWELLERY.

GOVERNMENT. Although Saudi Arabia is ruled by a king, the country is not a monarchy in the Western sense. Unlike other hereditary systems of government, succession in Saudi Arabia is not based on primogeniture; instead, senior members of the Al-Saudi family consult with each other and decide which of them is best suited to be Crown Prince and then King. All the kings to date have been sons of Abdul Aziz, the founder of the modern Saudi state.

G

The official government emblem is the palm tree over crossed swords. The palm symbolizes vitality, growth, and prosperity, while the swords represent strength and justice. This emblem is also used by members of the Royal Family, whether or not they hold government positions.

The Saudi method of ruling is a synthesis of traditional values which includes, first and foremost, a commitment to the teachings of Islam, followed by lineage and strong leadership. It is the duty of the king as both religious and secular leader, to ensure an ongoing compatibility between faith and government. In a region which has a history of political volatility, the leadership of the Al-Saud family has been a record of unbroken peace and stability. This can be attributed to a system of government which, overall, responds to the needs of the people.

The king also carries the titles of Prime Minister and Commander-in-Chief of the Armed Forces. King Fahd added the title Custodian of the Two Holy Mosques. The king appoints the Crown Prince who serves as First Deputy Prime Minister.

Twenty ministries deal with all executive matters. Saudi Arabia's 14 provinces are administered by a governor (*amir*) and regional officers. Local advisory councils appointed by

Saudi Arabian Government Departments

G

National Guard
Ministry of Defence and Aviation
Ministry of Interior
Ministry of Foreign Affairs
Ministry of Petroleum and Mineral Resources
Ministry of Finance and National Economy
Ministry of Municipalities and Rural Affairs
Ministry of Housing and Public Works
Ministry of Higher Education
Ministry of Education
Presidency of Women's Education
Ministry of Hajj
Ministry of Islamic Affairs
Ministry of Labour and Social Affairs
Ministry of Communications
Ministry of Justice
Ministry of Information
Ministry of Posts, Telegraphs, and Telephones
Ministry of Industry and Electricity
Ministry of Commerce
Ministry of Health
Ministry of Agriculture
Ministry of Planning
Presidency of Youth Welfare

the king and headed by the governor consist of officials and at least 10 private citizens with special areas of expertise. There is a total of 20 members who sit on each council. Various subcommittees concentrate on specific issues relating to the province. Reports from provincial councils go to the Ministry of Interior which then passes them to appropriate agencies for action. *See also* CONSULTATIVE COUNCIL; COUNCIL OF MINISTERS; MAJLIS; ROYAL DIWAN.

H

HAIL. Hail (pronounced 'hile') is the name given to both the province and its capital city. This northern region of Saudi Arabia lies on the southern border of the Nafud desert. The lofty mountains of Jabal Shammar, Jabal Aja, and Jabal Selma impose themselves on the nearby horizons.

Settlement of the otherwise arid terrain was only possible because deep aquifers allowed sustainable agriculture. For bedouins, pilgrims, and commercial caravans travelling across the harsh desert routes, this verdant oasis must have been a welcome sight. Lady Anne Blunt, author of *A Pilgrimage to Najd*, visited Hail in 1878. The region captivated her: *I feel that we have achieved something which is not given to everyone to do.*

Much evidence indicates that Hail has been inhabited for thousands of years. Moqaq, a farming region 60 kilometres west of the capital, is particularly rich in archaeological sites with ancient writings and drawings. Scholars are still trying to decipher some of the unfamiliar scripts.

Hail's strategic position on the trade routes between the Arabian Gulf and Damascus and, later, from the northern regions to Riyadh, helped the city to prosper as a market centre and provisioning post.

Until the early part of the 20th century, Hail was the stronghold of the Al-Rashids, once the formidable enemies of the Al-Sauds. They had a notoriously bloody history: eight of the nine Al-Rashid rulers were murdered by relatives.

As in the past, the region's principal activity is agriculture. Thanks to numerous government incentives and the construction of dams, more than 350,000 acres are currently under cultivation. Production has now diversified from the traditional crops of dates and grains to include fruits and olives. New strains of crops have been developed to better cope with the region's climate. The improved quality and increased quantity of agricultural products are now exported to other parts of the Kingdom.

Commercial and industrial activities, too, have grown in recent years, partly as offshoots of the agricultural industry and partly in response to fledgling tourism.

HAJJ. The fifth pillar of Islam requires Muslims to make a pilgrimage (*hajj*) to Makkah at least once in their lifetime if they are physically and financially able. This duty must be performed during specified days (9-12 *Dhu al-Hijah* in the Islamic *hejira* calendar) and according to specified rituals: *tawaf* (circling the *ka'ba* seven times), *saiy* (striving), *wukuf* (the most important part of the *hajj*. Pilgrims gather at Arafat to pray, meditate, and listen to sermons before proceeding to the hill of Muzdalifah at sunset), and *jamarat* (throwing seven stones, gathered at Muzdalifah, at three pillars, 'the satans', at Mina).

During the performance of *hajj*, all believers are equal, as symbolised by the large, unseamed white fabric wrapped around the waist and hung across the shoulder of each man. Women who make the pilgrimage must remain unveiled.

Approximately two million Muslims come to Makkah each

year during the *hajj* period. All pilgrims must register with a guide (*mutawwif*) who is responsible for them during their stay. He assists the pilgrim concerning food, water, transport, and accommodation. *See also* FIVE PILLARS OF ISLAM; UMRAH.

HAJJI. A *hajji* is the person who fulfills the obligations of the *hajj*, the pilgrimage that is the obligation of all Muslims. Henna-dyed hair and beard on a male Muslim indicates he has performed *hajj,* although not all male pilgrims distinguish themsleves in this way. In earlier times, pilgrims commonly

Two pilgrims wearing* ihram *pray during their* hajj *to Makkah.

dyed the manes of donkeys that had accompanied them on the journey.

HAMOUR. This meaty, flavourful member of the grouper family is considered by locals to be the Rolls Royce of edible fish. Whole *hamour* often appear as the centrepiece of buffets.

HAWTAH. Throughout Arabia the name *hawtah* or *hautah* appears, as in Hawtah Beni Tamim, near the ibex reserve south of Al-Kharj. *Hawtah*, Arabic for 'reserve', is akin to *hima* but is frequently associated, especially in South Arabia, with sacred groves or enclaves set aside in ancient times for ritual hunting. *See also* HIMA.

HEJIRA. The *hejira* refers to the emigration of the Prophet Muhammad from Makkah to Madina in AD 622. Having lost the patronage of the main clan in Makkah, Muhammad negotiated protection from the main Arab tribes in Madina during the pilgrimage of June 622. He and his followers moved to Madina in the following September.

Muslim dates are given according to the *hejira* calendar. The *hejira* era does not begin on the date of Muhammad's arrival in Madina but on the first day of the lunar year in which that happened: 16 July AD 622. *See also* HEJIRA CALENDAR.

HEJIRA CALENDAR. Saudis refer primarily to the *hejira* calendar. Unlike the Gregorian calendar, which is based on the rotation of the earth around the sun, the *hejira* months follow the movements of the moon.

The lunar calendar has 12 months of 28-30 days, or 354 days per year. Depending on the sightings of the new moons, the lunar year is generally 11 days shorter than the 365-day solar year. If, for example, the new year begins on 15 March in 2002, it will start on 4 March in 2003. Unlike other lunar calendars, the Islamic one does not add a 13th month. The *hejira* months therefore do not keep in line with the seasons.

The Muslim calendar was begun by Caliph Omar. It takes its starting point from 16 July AD 622, the first day of the lunar year in which the Prophet Muhammed and his followers fled from Makkah to Madina to escape persecution. Thus, the year AD 2002 corresponds to AH (*anno hejira*) 1422/1423. The longer solar year accounts for the slight discrepancy between the first *hejira* year and the current Gregorian year.

Because the term 'AD' (*Anno Domini*) conflicts with Muslim beliefs, Gregorian years are often referred to as 'CE' (Christian Era).

The 12 Muslim months are: Muharram, Safar, Rabi' I (Rabi' Al-Awwal), Rabi' II (Rabi' Ath-Thani), Jumadi I (Jumadi al-Ula), Jumadi II (Jumadi al-Akhirah), Rajab, Sha'ban, Ramadan, Shawwal, Dhu al-Qida, and Dhu al-Hijjah. *See also* HEJIRA.

HENNA. One of henna's most widespread functions is as a hair treatment. The colourant strengthens hair and gives it a silken sheen. Because henna does not penetrate the hair shaft, it is harmless to both scalp and hair if applied correctly. Henna mixed with dried black limes dyes hair black. Henna is not suitable for light-coloured or grey hair.

Henna is also used as a dye and moisturizer for the soles of the feet and the palms and backs of the hands. When mixed with egg and applied to toe- and fingernails, it acts as a strengthening agent. Some tribes believe that henna spread over exposed surfaces keeps the body cool in summer.

Henna also has decorative appeal. Dried, finely ground henna leaves are mixed with a small amount of water or

The night before her wedding, a young bride's hands are intricately decorated with henna.

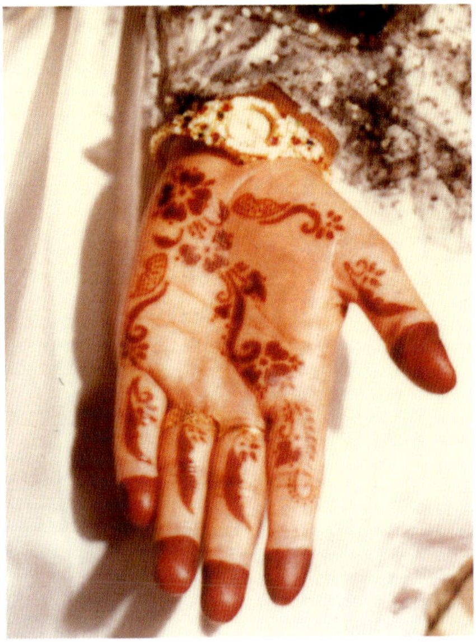

H

eucalyptus oil and strained lemon juice to form an elastic consistency. The henna artist then paints the moist henna onto the skin in floral or geometric designs with a toothpick or needle or a device like a pastry cone. This is a specialized, time-consuming art.

For the less artistic, *suqs* sell ready-made patterns for tracing designs onto the hands. A coating of mustard oil or a blend of lemon juice, sugar, pepper, and garlic gently swabbed onto the painted areas prevents the drying henna from flaking and intensifies the colour. The stain can last for as long as four weeks if the painted areas remain undisturbed for approximately five hours after the application. The dye should not become wet for the first 12 hours after scraping off the henna. During this period the colour becomes stronger.

HIJAZ. This is the name given to the western part of Saudi Arabia. The Hijaz is not a province. It loosely comprises the area between Yanbu and Taif. The meaning of the word, 'barrier', refers to the region's north-south range of mountains which can reach heights of 3,000 metres. Ancient caravan routes travelled along the less treacherous eastern side of the Hijaz mountains where the valleys support many oasis settlements. Torrential runoffs on the western Hijaz traditionally made agriculture tenuous, although some farming occurs on the narrow Tihama plain. The construction of dams has helped to improve the situation.

With its proximity to Europe and the Levant, the Hijaz has always been known for its mercantile activities. Jeddah is recognised as the commercial capital of Saudi Arabia.

Just as traders flocked to this region, so did invaders. Although political power shifted to other regional centres such as Damascus, Baghdad, and Cairo in the middle of the 7th century AD, Makkah and Madina retained their spiritual prominence. There was much prestige in controlling these areas. The Sherifs of Jordan, the Fatimid and Mameluke dynasties of Egypt, and the Turkish Ottomans at various times ruled Hijaz. The Turks were the last foreigners to exert their influence on the region (from the 16th-20th century) before King Abdul Aziz took control in 1926.

The main cities in the Hijaz are Jeddah, Makkah, Madina, Taif, and Yanbu. *See also* JEDDAH; MAKKAH; MADINA; TAIF; YANBU.

HIJAZ RAILWAY. Through rather unusual circumstances, the Hijaz Railway is prominent among history's more famous routes. The actual operation of the line was relatively short lived (nine years); ironically, it was its destruction in 1917 by the legendary T.E. Lawrence – Lawrence of Arabia – and his Arab followers which has brought the route immortality.

The idea for a rail route connecting Damascus and

Madina and, eventually, the Yemen, was first discussed in 1897, ostensibly as a means of facilitating pilgrim travel to and from Islam's most revered shrines. Where the caravan route took 40 nights between Damascus and Madina, the same distance would take only three nights by rail. This concept coincided with rumours about the British building a railroad from Port Said to an undetermined port on the eastern coast of Arabia. The political ramifications of a possible strengthening of the British position in the Middle East were untenable for the Ottomans so the project was subtly discouraged.

Insurrections in 1898 by the Imam of Yemen, together with skirmishes in central Arabia, forced the Sultan to reconsider his options. A train would provide speedier communications over difficult and potentially dangerous terrain. Furthermore, it might be easier to keep the railway line functioning in winter when other important land routes became impassable. Not wanting to risk the loss of the holy cities of Makkah and Madina because of their obvious religious and strategic significance, and also wanting to strengthen his influence in the Hijaz, Sultan Abdul Hamid II was induced to resurrect the project but he did so under innovative terms.

Emphasizing the religious rather than military, political, or economic aspects, the Sultan decided to fund the entire construction from private subscription from all parts of the Islamic world. To supplement the financial requirements he later imposed various taxes.

The construction project began in 1900. A German engineer, Meissner, oversaw a team of 43 international engineers. It is worth noting that none was from England or the US. More than 5,000 Turks, Syrians, and Iraqis carried out the manual labour.

The railway covered a distance of 1,609 kilometres. There was a total of 52 stopping places about 34 kilometres apart, or the equivalent of a day's march. For both political and financial reasons, the railway never went further than Madina. Even that distance, however, was a tremendous benefit to pilgrims. Not only were their travel expenses reduced significantly but the journey was immensely more comfortable. Camel caravan owners, needless to say, were displeased with the lost revenue. Their frequent attacks on the trains meant that it wasn't always safer to travel by train than by caravan.

Each station had its own character. Some had a distinctly European look to them. The name of one station, Al-Badaya, comes from an Arabic word meaning 'magnificent'. It was built in mock Gothic style, somewhat resembling a crusader castle.

A Turkish locomotive blown up by the forces of the Arab Revolt, with the support and assistance of T.E. Lawrence.

In Saudi Arabia little of the railway remains but this does not stop travellers from getting into their four-wheel drive vehicles and making the rugged journey through the desert to retrace the route. The derelict sheds, abandoned stations, and sometimes parts of, or a whole, train lying by the ghosts of the tracks stimulate the imagination and, like all great railways, conjure up romantic notions of a lost era.

HIMA. The concept of setting aside areas around settlements and protecting them from grazing was once practised throughout Arabia. Prophet Muhammed established *himas* around Madina and enshrined the ancient tribal custom in Islamic law.

In addition to the need to protect food-growing areas from the depredations of nomadic peoples' flocks, increasing aridity made resources scarce; the need to husband vital food sources became imperative. The system gave villagers rights over the land around their settlements. Some of the early Caliphs instituted strict punishments for cutting even a single branch from such a reserve.

The *hima* was usually administered by the *muhtasib* (person in charge of establishing good and forbidding evil in society). Later, particularly in the Hijaz, it was administered by the local chief of a tribe or village; fines were paid in the form of livestock in graduated penalties, depending on the frequency of the offense.

There were five types of *hima* identified in western Saudi Arabia in the 1960s: areas in which grazing was prohibited but the cutting of fodder was permitted during drought years; areas where grazing and cutting were permitted on a seasonal basis after the flowering of grass and other plants; areas where grazing was allowed but limited to certain types of animals; areas primarily for beekeeping; and areas to protect trees. There were also areas set aside to protect a particular species of mammal, such as Jabal Ral near Al-Wijh, described as an ibex reserve by local inhabitants and established as recently as 200 years ago.

The size of *himas* varied from a hectare to several thousand square kilometres. In the Asir, virtually every village was associated with one or more *himas*, largely because the terraced agriculture demanded extensive pastures to feed the draught animals.

There were estimated to be 3,000 *himas* in the Kingdom in 1965. Many disappeared at the end of King Abdul Aziz's reign when a royal decree abolished the royal *himas* he had established to provide fodder for the cavalry. This ruling was interpreted to apply to all *himas*.

The decline of the *hima* has had a devastating effect on vegetation. The consequent denudation of plant cover has led to serious soil erosion which, in association with severe floods, has led to the destruction of old systems of soil and water conservation using terraces. Many experts feel that *himas* should continue to be encouraged and extended as they are an excellent way of preserving rare species of animals and plants and of regulating the use of renewable resources. Moreover, they are an indigenous system, firmly routed in the religious and cultural value system of the Saudi people. *See also* HAWTAH.

HOFUF. As the principal city in the famous date-producing oasis of Al-Ahsa, it is to be expected that Hofuf's main activities centre around dates: bulk markets with an annual turnover of one million kilos of dates, processing plants, and even a university that devotes itself to date research.

Hofuf is equally famous for camels. An important camel research centre on the outskirts of the city also provides veterinary services. Many tribes pass through the area to attend the weekly camel market each Thursday morning from dawn to 0900h. This is a favourite outing for photographers and expatriates who would like to experience the thrill of riding a camel.

Other markets in Hofuf are the covered market and the women's *suq*. They sell everything from frankincense and shepherds' staffs to dresses and mattresses. Handmade metal objects and bedouin weavings are available here.

The 19th century fort Qasr Ibrahim was originally built by the Turks. A mosque, dating from about 1566, was the first building on the site, followed by a 17th century fort that was rebuilt in the 19th century. King Abdul Aziz captured the fort in 1913. A site permit issued by the Department of Antiquities in Riyadh, is required in order to visit the fort.

Hofuf's museum, called the Al-Ahsa Museum of Archaeology and Ethnography, gives a comprehensive look at the region's archaeological history and cultural traditions. Explanations are written in English and Arabic. Admission is free but it is only open from Saturday to Wednesday.

Sitated 385 kilometres east of Riyadh and 125 kilometres west of Dammam, Hofuf makes an easy and pleasant weekend excursion. *See also* AL-AHSA; DATE; POTTERY.

HONEY/BEEKEEPING. The Kingdom's best honey comes from the southwest region where diverse and profuse vegetation give the honey an interesting flavour.

Connoisseurs test the purity of honey by using a matchstick to draw out a sample. If, for even a second, the ribbon of honey breaks its flow, it is deemed to have been diluted with other substances. Some unscrupulous beekeepers adulterate the end product by feeding their bees sugar syrup. This increases the yield but reduces the quality. Even the ordinary retail customer can distinguish the high quality honey from the regular commercial brands: tip the jar upside down and notice how the thickness of the Saudi honey slows the flow.

In addition to the gastronomic pleasure of eating the unique, rich Arabian honey, locals swear by its medicinal benefits: old men take a spoonful each day to retain their youth, young men take it in the hope of producing sons, and women who have given birth take honey to quickly regain their strength.

HOSPITALITY. Hospitality is an inherent feature of Saudi tradition. Arabia's harsh environment and the predominantly nomadic lifestyle of previous generations made the custom one of necessity in a fight for survival: a person able to offer hospitality today might be in dire need of it himself tomorrow.

The bedouin have such a reputation for generosity that an enemy who enters the encampment in peace can remain as a privileged guest for three days before being asked his name or the purpose of his visit. The 'bond of salt' puts the guest under the protection of the host, not just for the time of his visit but for three days after his departure. The expression *When you offer hospitality, pour riches* reflects the willingness of the bedouin to give the best they have to a guest, although it could mean deprivation for the family. The honour of generosity is an important facet of the Arab personality.

Even in modern urban society, an almost sacred observance of the unwritten rules of hospitality persists.

HOUBARA. This migratory bustard (*Chlamydotis undulata macqueenii*) ranges between the Sinai desert and western Mongolia. The birds winter in the deserts of Arabia. In addition, there is a small, endangered resident population within the Kingdom.

In captivity, houbara mate between the ages of one and six years. In the courtship ritual, the male offers a showy display of his open neck ruff as he leaps and struts, hoping to attract a potential mate's attention. Females lay between one and four eggs (two to three eggs is average) in a scooped out hollow in the sand. The eggs hatch after a period of approximately 23 days.

Because of its feisty nature, the turkey-like houbara is a favourite prey for falconers. Hunting, overgrazing, and the

The beady eye of a Houbara Bustard keeps a lookout for danger.

expansion of urban and agricultural areas brought the birds to the verge of extinction in Saudi Arabia.

A successful captive breeding programme run by the National Commission for Wildlife Conservation and Development in Taif is helping to halt the decline in numbers and restock the wild population. The protected areas that NCWCD has established at Mahazat As-Sayd and Harrat Al-Harrah make the houbara less vulnerable during migration and also help to protect the resident populations. Nevertheless, legal but unpoliced hunting practices continue to put the houbara at risk.

HUBBLY-BUBBLY. *See* SHISHA.

I

I

IBEX. In Saudi Arabia, the Nubian ibex (*Capra ibex nubiana*) makes its habitat in the Asir highlands and the rugged sandstone Tuwaig escarpment which winds from the northern edge of the Empty Quarter northwards to the northern portion of central Saudi Arabia. Nubian ibex have roamed the Arabian peninsula since the last Ice Age. They have been the prey of hunters since neolithic times, as evidenced by numerous cave drawings and petroglyphs. Modern man threatened the existence of Nubian ibex in Arabia due to overgrazing and indiscriminate hunting. In order to protect and preserve the species, the National Commission for Wildlife Conservation and Development (NCWCD) has set aside several special reserves. The most noteable of these is the Hawtat Bani Tamiim, an area of 2,400 square kilometres about 200 kilometres south of Riyadh.

These magnificent mountain goats are well suited to their environment. In a landscape known for its sparse vegetation, ibex can eat a wide variety of plants, some of which are toxic to other animals. Their keen senses of smelling and hearing and their agility at rapidly scaling steep, rocky cliffs and running along precipitous ledges help them to evade predators.

A fully-grown male can weigh as much as 100 kilos, twice as much as the female. The male's horns, more curved and with more prominent knots than the female's, can reach one metre in length. Males use their horns as a threat against other males but sometimes the only way to establish dominance within the herd is actual head-butting combat.

Mating occurs mainly in October, although it may continue until mid-November. After a gestation period of 150-163 days, females retreat to a remote refuge to give birth in March/April. Twins are not uncommon. Females remain with their young for three-four weeks until the kids are strong and sure-footed enough to join the rest of the herd.

IGAAL. The black, braided cord is doubled over and sits on the *ghutra* or *shama'agh*, the head covering worn by Saudi men. The *igaal* was originally used to hobble camels. King Abdul Aziz and senior tribal and government officials wore a more elaborate *igaal* with three tiers of cord bound together with gold thread and a tassle down the back. King Faisal was the last Saudi monarch to wear this style.

IMAM. *See* ISLAM.

INCENSE. In the Arab world, incense represents expressions of both welcome and farewell and is a salient segment of important ceremonies or the recognition of special guests. When the gently smoking incense burner is passed, each person fans the redolent wisps of smoke into the hair and clothing where the pleasant aroma can linger for several days.

Frankincense and myrrh are gum-resins that have been popular for more than 6,000 years. Once exposed to heat, the semi-opaque lumps exude a balsamic odor. In historical times, those who could afford it used myrrh as a sacred anointing oil and an embalming fluid, and for cooking and fumigation. Frankincense and myrrh are still used to keep pests away and to purify water and, in remote areas, for a variety of medicinal and cosmetic purposes. Sandalwood, a wood which comes primarily from India, is another popular fragrance. The most expensive incenses can cost thousands of riyals for relatively small amounts.

A lovely Arabic saying expresses the wish, *Incense so you will return.*

INCENSE BURNER. Incense burners (*mubkhara*) are crafted from a number of materials, including unbaked clay, wood, stone, or metals. The basic shape of the *mubkhara* has remained unchanged for more than 2,000 years: a square base mounted on four legs supports a square receptacle for small pieces of incense which are placed on several lumps of glowing charcoal.

Contemporary Saudis usually choose imported models made from metals such as aluminium, brass, silver, or gold. In Saudi Arabia, only in Hail, a city 700 kilometres north of

A typical bedouin incense burner, made of wood with columns covered in lead and decorated with brass tacks and mirrors.

Riyadh, are *mubkhara* still made in the traditional manner. Using hand-forged tools, local craftsmen carve censers from solid blocks of tamarisk wood, a process which takes an average of six days. Decorative touches can include bronze studs, brass sheeting with geometric designs, and small mirrors, a throwback to primitive superstitions which held that reflective objects repel evil spirits.

IQAMA. Legally employed foreign residents must carry an identity document called an *iqama* with them at all times. Dependents can carry either a copy of the information pages from their passports or a photocopy of the employee's *iqama* which lists accompanying family members.

ISLAM. In Saudi Arabia, Islam is not merely a religion but also a way of life. Its tenets guide all aspects of society, setting down codes of behaviour that include the most general and the most specific situations.

Islam means 'submission' and, in Saudi Arabia particularly, this submission to God's will is absolute. The Western concept of state remaining separate from religion is alien to Islam.

According to Islamic belief, the angel Gabriel began transmitting God's teachings to the Prophet Muhammad near Makkah in AD 610. The *Qur'an* documents these inspired revelations and is Islam's irrefutable source of reference. Further moral guidance comes from the *sunnah*. This is a collection of Prophet Muhammad's sayings and examples, each of which is referred to as a *hadith*. Muhammad himself is called the Seal of the Prophets (*khatim al-anbiya'*). He is the last in a line from Adam, through Noah, Abraham , Moses, and Jesus.

The Muslim place of worship is called the mosque (*masjid*). Islam has no ordained clergy. Anyone may lead communal prayers but in the mosque it is usually an *imam* (meaning 'in front'), a religious figure who performs this function and who delivers a sermon (*khutbah*) at the Friday noon prayer.

Makkah and Madina are Islam's holiest sites; only Muslims are allowed within the two cities' areas of sanctuary. Besides the fact that the Prophet Muhammad came from Makkah, the city has special prominence because it is here that the *ka'ba* is located. Tradition holds that the Prophet Abraham and his son Ishmael laid its foundation. The building, situated in the centre courtyard of the Grand Mosque, is Islam's most sacred shrine.

Every Muslim has five religious obligations: profession of faith, prayer, almsgiving, fasting, and pilgrimage. As well as living their lives within these five pillars of faith, Muslims have certain dietary restrictions: they may not consume intoxicating beverages, pork, blood, or animals which have not been slaughtered according to Islamic ritual. Foods which contain even minute percentages of forbidden ingredients are also forbidden. These include some gelatins and all products made with alcohol, such as pure vanilla extract.

Two main Muslim sects exist: the majority *Sunni*, or traditionalists, and the minority (about 10 per cent) *Shia* (sometimes referred to as *Shi'ite*) whose name derives from the Arabic for 'partisans' (of Ali). Although both branches share the same fundamental beliefs, they differ markedly in political and structural orientation.

By example and strength of character, the Prophet Muhammad was able to unify his followers, regardless of their tribal loyalties. Ironically, it was his death which caused discord and division. Muhammad left no appointed successor. One faction, which became known as *Sunni*, believed that the *khalifa* (successor) should be elected from the believers. Opposing Muslims, the *Shia*, maintained that Muhammad's cousin and son-in-law, Ali, should be his religious heir, and claimed he had been named as such by the Prophet Muhammad. The verbal conflict led to the AD 680 rebellion of Ali's followers against the ruling caliph and resulted in a massacre of the attackers. *See also* FIVE PILLARS OF ISLAM; MOSQUE; QUR'AN; RAMADAN; WAHHIBISM.

ISLAMIC BANKING. Islam sets out guidelines for every aspect of a Muslim's life. Monetary issues are no exception but, until recently, the strong influence of interest-based institutions has generally prevailed over Islamically-acceptable systems of finance. Now, with more than 800 million Muslims in the world, an international debt-ridden economy, and the clear Qur'anic injunction against usury (*ribh*) demanding to be addressed, economists have begun to look to Islamic banking for some much-needed answers.

To the uninformed, Islamic banking means 'no interest given by the bank, no interest paid to the borrower.' In a society conditioned to receiving money for money, the Islamic approach has little appeal and would seem to have limited chance of success. Closer investigation, however, reveals that *Sharia* rulings on monetary matters are brilliantly logical, a view supported by economists all over the world.

The main difference between the prevailing interest system and the Islamic system is that the world's financial institutions trade money as a commodity. Money has an advance price which has no relation to its proposed function. Funds are lent on the strength of guarantees, not on the worthiness of the intended investment. The risks taken by banks and other lending institutions are of a financial nature, i.e. the risk of non-repayment, inflation, etc. Such a system makes the rich richer by favouring supposedly credit-worthy borrowers with lower interest rates.

Islamic banks, on the other hand, take business risks. They agree to take a percentage of the outcome rather than the capital. In Islam, the bank is a partner. By the same token, the depositor, too, is a partner. Through his deposits, he participates in the activities of the bank and shares in the bank's profits or losses, according to the percentage deposited. Thus, according to Islamic concepts, the way to reduce credit is not by imposing controls but by profit and loss sharing. On this basis, bankers will look more carefully at a project to judge its suitability.

The nature of Islamic banking is also the challenge facing it. Although there is a large sympathy to work without interest, technically such a programme is difficult to implement given the influence of interest institutions and the infrastructure necessary to make Islamic banks perform to their full benefit. While interest-based institutions reduce financial uncertainties by establishing central banks, legislation, codes of deposits, liquidity ratios, etc., Islamic banks must yet find suitable ways to minimize business risks. Primarily, this depends upon professionally-trained personnel acquainted with a wide range of business environments. It also requires proper financial resources and ways to service surplus liquidity. Non-risk money cannot be used in risk ventures. It therefore becomes necessary to change the nature of money and educate people to become more willing to participate in entrepreneurial ventures.

J

J

JAMBIA. This traditional dagger is encased in a sharply curved sheath covered with decorated silver or other metal, or with tooled leather. It can take several months to craft some of the more ornate sheaths. The handles are often made from bone but also can be metal. A leather or colourfully embroidered belt holds the dagger in place.

Though not as important as swords in battle, daggers are most probably older and were used not only as weapons but more frequently as an accessory to a man's costume. Today, the *jambia* is often worn at official or ceremonial functions by men who might not otherwise wear it as a regular addition to their clothing. In the southwest regions of the Kingdom, many men, particularly the older generation, continue to wear *jambias* on a daily basis.

JANADRIYA. Janadriya, a large plain about 30 kilometres northeast of Riyadh, was originally the site of a major annual camel race organized by the National Guard. In 1984, in order to strengthen the links with the country's past, the concept was expanded to include a heritage festival. The ever increasing area now covers more than 50 square kilometres and attracts nearly 2 million visitors annually.

Janadriya is devoted to a two-week exhibition of Saudi culture representative of all parts of the Kingdom. Visitors can see traditional crafts being plied right before their eyes. The area includes displays of perfume making, basket weaving, tailoring, metal work, and pottery. To add to the ambiance, camels and donkeys perform at tasks such as working a sesame oil press or pulling carts. Other entertainment includes traditional games and sports.

As well as cultural heritage, the exhibition illustrates the Kingdom's recent history. Government bodies provide special displays to inform the public of ongoing activities.

In the evenings, folklore shows attract large crowds. Dancers and musicians from around the country perform at the specially created grandstand. The festival is also a gathering place for leading poets and thinkers who participate in literary gatherings and symposia.

Fitting in comfortably with the Kingdom's rich heritage, the camel races continue. Now more than 2,000 animals participate.

JEDDAH. This sprawling metropolis sits snugly on the narrow coastal plain between the Red Sea on the west and the Hijaz mountain range to the east. As Saudi Arabia's main port on the Red Sea and the gateway to the pilgrimage destinations of Makkah and Madina, Jeddah has always enjoyed a special prominence and a cosmopolitan buzz that is absent in other

Saudi cities. Until the mid 1980s diplomatic representatives based themselves in Jeddah, despite the fact that Riyadh has always been the Kingdom's administrative capital. The city remains Saudi Arabia's cultural and commercial capital and home to many of the country's most important trading families.

The word Jeddah comes from the Arabic *jedda* meaning 'grandmother'. Legend has it, and an actual grave gives substance to the legend, that Eve is buried in Jeddah. This, despite the fact that current archaeological evidence of early settlement only goes back about 2,000 years. For most of its history, its strategic location half way down the Red Sea coast

In the commercial heart of Jeddah, the National Commercial Bank's headquarters dominates the skyline.

and on the ancient caravan routes has ensured prosperity. At various times, it has been ruled by caliphs in Makkah, the Mameluke dynasty of Egypt, and the Ottoman Empire. King Abdul Aziz took control in 1925.

Modern Jeddah, called 'The Bride of the Red Sea', is famous for its corniche and its more than 400 outdoor sculptures. The city also boasts the world's tallest fountain, situated in the sea opposite the Al-Salam Palace. Like most coastal cities, Jeddah's atmosphere is more relaxed that that of inland communities. Beaches, boating, and water sports give residents added recreational opportunities.

Unlike many other places in the Kingdom, Jeddah has been keen to preserve parts of its old city (Al-Balad). Some of the buildings, which once belonged to wealthy merchant families, have been turned into museums. Some of the oldest houses were constructed out of coral; others have interesting idiosyncracies attached to their construction: in Naseef House, where King Abdul Aziz stayed after capturing Jeddah, the stairway is wide enough for a camel to carry loads of water from the ground level to the seventh floor. One of the most unusual museums is that of Abdel Raouf Hasan Khalil. Its four buildings comprise an eclectic hodge-podge of more than 10,000 weird and wonderful artefacts.

JEWELLERY. Saudi women, particularly the bedouin, love to adorn themselves with jewellery. In this society, jewellery is more than mere fashion; it also indicates status and, in times of need, provides a useful source of cash.

Gold jewellery is sold by weight; design is of relatively little value. Each piece is set on a gram scale and priced according to the international daily rate for gold. Western-styled gold jewellery usually comes from Italy. More ornate pieces are fashioned locally.

Jewellery is a customary dowry item. ‘Wedding sets’, referred to as royal jewellery sets (*taqm malaki*) comprise a necklace, bracelet, ring, earrings, and accessory pin in gold studded with diamonds and/or other precious stones. While the gold jewellery is often similar in design to that found in the West, the bedouin styles are unique.

Islam forbids Muslim men to wear gold. It is common, though, for men to wear a silver ring with a round, unfaceted and often unpolished stone. *See also* BEDOUIN JEWELLERY; DESERT DIAMONDS.

JIZAN. Saudi Arabia is a land of many contrasts: geographical, cultural, and environmental. Perhaps nowhere is this more evident than in the Kingdom’s southwest province of Jizan.

Encompassing only 15,457 square kilometres, Jizan ranks as the Kingdom’s second smallest province. Yet this relatively limited amount of space does not lack diversity. Coastal salt flats gradually give way to lush plains and magnificent mountains. Countless small *wadis* (dry river beds) and approximately 20 main *wadis* rest peacefully between these mountains. The province even has two extinct volcanoes. Locals call them Al-Garatayn, meaning ‘the two barrens’, because nothing grows on them.

Despite its small size, Jizan boasts the Kingdom’s greatest population density: 26 people per square kilometre, compared with only three people per square kilometre in Riyadh, the country’s capital. Such a high concentration is due to the fact that Jizan has 70 per cent of the Kingdom’s naturally arable land, earning Jizan the title ‘breadbasket of Saudi Arabia’. While other provinces now have large agricultural developments, much of this is the result of land reclamation and soil additives. Jizan’s soil, exceptionally rich in micro-elements, can successfully grow several crops per year without chemical assistance.

Jizan's culture is as lavish as its land. Located beside ancient caravan routes and ports, the region once profited from the trade and tuition of travellers. For centuries the province has enjoyed the worthy distinction of generating some of the Kingdom's finest literary figures.

Architecture in the province bears witness to the varied origins of its population. Here one can see the haystack-like huts of the Tihama which exude an African influence. Many pilgrims returning from Makkah decided to settle in Jizan rather than continue to their native lands. Because the coastal plains provided no stone for building, the new settlers resorted to their familiar methods of using mud and straw. The insides of the huts often have white-washed walls and geometrically painted ceilings. Some also have decorative shelving for storage.

Neighbouring Yemen has left its imprint on the province with the introduction of bright colours in clothes and possessions, and houses faced with shiny ceramic tiles. Stone forts and finely detailed plasterwork are reminders of the Ottoman rule. The town of Farasan, on the out-islands of the same name, offers some of the best and most prolific examples of plaster-decorated buildings, as well as tantalizing possibilities of exciting archaeological finds.

The Farasans are one of the world's last remaining unspoiled banks of coral reef. Located about 20 kilometres off Jizan's coast, the bountiful underwater life almost defies description. The more than 100 uninhabited islands within Jizan's jurisdiction make tempting destinations. Officials are thus faced with the dual task of preserving the richness of the reef as well as improving and introducing the many facilities needed to cater to an influx of visitors.

For local colour and a look at trade as it has gone on for countless generations, an excursion to one of the weekly markets is a must. Main villages such as Abu Areesh, Al-Ardtha, and Sabya provide central locations to which the smaller villages contribute a cornucopia of goods. Even if profits prove disappointing, the animation of the marketplace provides a lively exchange of news and views in an otherwise placid existence.

In ancient times, Jizan's many mineral springs enjoyed regular patronage because of their curative powers. Only eight or nine of the original spas remain but officials are giving serious consideration to reopening them to the public as an attractive source of therapy and relaxation.

What nature has given in abundant beauty and wildlife, it has withheld in cooperative weather patterns. During summer, when people normally have long periods of vacation, the temperatures and humidity in Jizan reach uncomfortable levels. From late October to mid February, however, the pleasantly warm climate offers welcome respite from colder weather elsewhere. Nevertheless, with such a limited season, the province cannot afford to rely solely on tourism.

Although agriculture ranks foremost in development plans, the sea, too, is a major source of revenue. A local fishery company has expanded its export markets to include Japan and the US. Officials are looking into the possibility of establishing a mariculture industry. So great is the scope for such a project that Jizan could easily accommodate the entire Kingdom's seafood needs.

New and extensive support facilities allow the province to tap its vast resources and expand its prospects. The Wadi Jizan dam stands out as the most impressive of the province's many projects. Heavy rains in the mountains used to cause devastating flash floods which claimed numerous lives, swept away communities and caused serious erosion. Now the torrents from five wadis are channeled into the dam's reservoir for selective release.

JUBAIL. Of the Kingdom's many testaments to progress, perhaps none has been more ambitious than the creation of the twin industrial cities of Jubail on the Arabian Gulf and Yanbu on the Red Sea. There are indications that Jubail, meaning 'small mountain', was inhabited by Phoenicians as early as 3000 BC. Centrally situated on ancient trade routes, the town flourished for centuries, its success augmented by a lucrative pearling industry.

In the mid 1970s, in an effort to reduce the Kingdom's dependence upon crude oil exports, the government embarked on a major programme of industrialization. The main thrust of the operation centred on the country's two coasts. Jubail, in Saudi Arabia's Eastern Province, was an obvious choice because it is situated at the heart of the Kingdom's petroleum deposits and is close to deep navigable Gulf waters. To oversee the enormous undertaking, the government established the Royal Commission for Jubail and Yanbu.

The building of a physical infrastructure included ports, airports, more than 560 kilometres of roads, and utilities at the two sites. Extensive harbour facilities and easy access to international airports have contributed to Jubail's and Yanbu's status as powerful industrial cities.

Vital water supplies are provided by desalination plants which can produce up to 90,000 cubic metres of distilled water per day for Jubail. Such plentiful water is in sharp contrast to earlier years: in 1928 King Abd Al-Aziz ordered that a small fort be built to protect Jubail's only well. The seawater cooling systems have been designed so that water used by industries is recirculated and returned to source with minimal impact upon the environment. Thanks to the application of advanced technology and the implementation of strict controls, industrialization and environmental protection can successfully coexist at Jubail and Yanbu.

An equally important achievement has been the well-developed sense of community enjoyed by these modern, self-sufficient cities. The architects of the scheme have successfully blended traditional Saudi values with international living standards. Residents live in low-rise housing and each neighbourhood has its own mosques, hospital, schools for Arabic and non-Arabic-speaking pupils, sports and cultural facilities, and shopping areas. Nearly 500,000 people live in these communities.

Jubail, the larger of the twin cities, was the largest construction programme ever undertaken by the Kingdom. In fact, there can be few projects anywhere in the world that rival the magnitude of this endeavour. *See also* YANBU.

The desalination plant at Jubail, supplementing the region's supplies with the waters of the Gulf.

K

K

KA'BA. This 15-metre high strutcture located within the Grand Mosque in Makkah represents the spiritual and physical centre of Islam. As the first house of Allah on earth, it is the focal point for all Muslims. The name derives from the Arabic word for 'cube' because of the cube-like appearance of the building.

There are various stories concerning the origins of the *ka'ba*. The version written in the *Qur'an* is that Abraham (Ibrahim) and his son Ishmael (Ismail) constructed the foundation. Built into a corner of the *ka'ba* is a stone that believers say was given to Adam on his fall from paradise. Legend says the stone was originally white but has become black from all the sins of man that it has absorbed. Broken into three pieces during an attack on Makkah, the stone is held together and protected by a silver frame. A black silk cloth, intricately embroidered in gold and silver with excerpts from the *Qur'an* covers the *ka'ba*.

The *ka'ba* features prominently in the performance of the annual *hajj*. The faithful circle the *ka'ba* when they arrive in Makkah and when they complete their pilgrimage, as well as seven times during the *hajj* ritual: *When we prepared for Ibrahim the place of the House we said: 'Worship none beside me. Keep My House clean for those who walk around it and those who stand upright or kneel in worship.' Exhort all men to make the pilgrimage. They will come to you on foot and on the backs of swift camels from every distant quarter; they will come to avail themselves of many a benefit and to pronounce on the appointed days the name of Allah over the beasts which he has given them. Eat of their flesh yourselves, and feed the poor and unfortunate. Then let the pilgrims prepare themselves, make their vows, and circle the Ancient House. Such is Allah's commandment.* (22:22/29-30). *See also* HAJJ; KISWA.

KING FAHD CAUSEWAY. The opening of the King Fahd Causeway between the Arabian mainland and Bahrain in 1986 has made the nearby island state easily accessible to Saudis. It is not uncommon for a man to work in the Eastern Province and base his family in the less conservative environment of Bahrain, commuting back and forth. Weekend breaks to Bahrain have also increased in popularity.

This 25-kilometre long engineering marvel consists of a four-lane road and bridge link between Saudi Arabia and Bahrain. A manmade island in the centre of the causeway serves as the customs and immigration point for both countries. The project was funded entirely by Saudi Arabia.

A toll fee of 20 riyals is payable each way. Traffic is particularly heavy on Thursdays going to Bahrain and on Fridays going to Saudi Arabia. Buses have a special customs lane.

The customs post at the centre of the King Fahd Causeway lights up the night.

Exit/re-entry visas are required in order for non-Saudis to re-enter Saudi Arabia, even for a day-return trip. Drivers of Saudi-licensed cars are required to purchase temporary Bahrain insurance at the border.

KISWA. The *ka'ba* is covered with a black silk cloth (*kiswa*) that is intricately embroidered in gold and silver thread with text from the *Qur'an*. It is believed that this tradition began in AD 400. When the Prophet Muhammad conquered Makkah in AD 630, he performed *hajj* and covered the *ka'ba* with a *kiswa* made in Yemen. Egypt was also a source for the spectacular weavings. Under instructions from King Abdul Aziz, a factory in Makkah was constructed specifically for the purpose of producing the elegant coverings. *See also* KA'BA.

K

Craftsmen at work on the* kiswa *in Makkah.

KOHL. In Arabic, the word *kohl* refers to any substance that goes on the eyelid margin. Traditionally, it is a black powder usually made from antimony trisulphide or lead sulphide. Skilfully applied around the rims of the eyes, it gives Saudi women an exotic look.

Kohl has been popular for thousands of years in this part of the world, not only as a beauty preparation but also as medication. In former times it was used to prevent or fight eye infections. Its black, shiny properties were thought to shield the eyes from the glare and reflection of the sun. This probably influenced the belief that *kohl* cleared or improved vision.

The Prophet Muhammad encouraged the use of *kohl* but he specified the variety made from *ethmid*, a stone which consists mainly of antimony trisulphide. This inert substance does not irritate the mucous membranes. Today, because of the rarity of *ethmid*, most *kohl* contains 88 per cent lead sulphide concentration. It looks similar to *ethmid* but, as a toxic substance, it can cause many problems if introduced into the eye itself. One effect is chronic lead poisoning, particularly in children.

There are currently almost 30 different kinds of *kohl* on the market. Some include organic materials such as camphor or sandalwood. While certain types have proven antibacterial effects, many are heavily contaminated. Only highly reputable brands are recommended.

L

LABAN. A cultured yoghurt-type drink popular in Arabia before the advent of dairies, this refreshing, easily digested beverage was originally made from camel milk. Saudi Arabia's modern dairy industry was astonished to learn that the vast majority of their customers preferred *laban* to milk. Although the population has now been educated to drink increased quantities of milk, the preference for *laban* continues. *See also* DAIRIES.

LEGAL SYSTEM. *See* SHARIA.

LITERATURE. The Arabs are well known for their legendary ability to tell a good story and recite a moving poem with fervour. Yet for all the race's literary richness, *One Thousand and One Nights* is as close as most foreigners come to familiarizing themselves with Arabic masterpieces. Part of the reason for this is that the formal perfection of the Arabic language makes it one of the most difficult to translate effectively.

The Abbasid period (AD 750-1258) saw the first marked development in prose styles. The significant change in Arabic literature complemented the golden age of Iraq's Abbasid empire. The Iraqi intellectual Abu Uthman Amr bin Bahr Al-

Jahiz (AD 776-869) brought Arabic prose to heights of conciseness and clarity with his witty and insightful observations of human nature. The verbal virtuoso Badi' As-Zaman Al-Hamadhani (*d.*1008) invented a genre known as *maqamat* (assemblie). In these dramatic anecdotes, Al-Hamadhani displays an extraordinary command of vocabulary in his composition of amusing, elaborate rhymed prose.

After a long period of general decline between the mid 13th and late 19th centuries, Arabic literature began to make a come-back. By the early 20th century, Arab writers had started to depart from traditional florid methods of expression. Increasingly, authors drew on Arab situations and characters and dealt with Arab problems.

The Western world acknowledged the importance of Arabic literature when it awarded the Egyptian writer Naguib Mahfouz the Nobel Prize in 1988. Hopefully such recognition will inspire English-language readers to explore the rich world of Arabic literature beyond *One Thousand and One Nights*. *See also* POETRY.

LOOMI (DRIED LIMES). Either powdered or whole, this ingredient is a common flavouring in Gulf cooking. The limes dry naturally on the trees. *Loomi* can be added to soups and stews, mixed with fried onions and garlic, or rubbed on meat or poultry before grilling.

M

M

MADAIN SALEH. Of the many archaeological sites now under the protection of the Department of Antiquities, Madain Saleh (cities of Saleh) is the most imposing and perhaps the most mysterious.

Madain Saleh lies 420 kilometres northwest of Madina. The constantly changing landscape saves the rugged five-hour drive from monotony. Flat desert suddenly gives way to towering outcroppings of sandstone and to tall walls of basalt which mark the perimeters of ancient lava flows. Then, in a wide, sandy valley, the massive façades of ancient Nabataean tombs become visible. Surrounded by such tangible relics of achievement, visitors cannot fail to be impressed. Little is known about pre-historic Madain Saleh, or Al-Hijr as it is called locally by its more ancient name. Greek and Roman writers record that there were settled communities in the area for more than 3,000 years, starting with the Minaeans and succeeded by Thamudic, Lihyanite, and Nabataean occupations. Only the Nabataeans left their architectural stamp.

The Nabataeans originated in the Hijaz, the western part of the Arabian peninsula. As the tribe grew stronger, it made its way north, eventually settling in Petra in 500 BC. Within

200 years they controlled an extensive portion of the lucrative caravan route between Yemen and Rome. They occupied Madain Saleh, the southern capital of the settlements, from 9 BC to AD 106.

The Nabataeans amassed great wealth by imposing a 25 per cent tax on merchandise. In return for the hefty toll, they ensured safe travel by rigidly policing the route within their territory. Equally important, they used their mastery of hydraulic engineering to supply fresh water to the thirsty caravans. When the incense traders abandoned overland routes in favour of faster, less costly sea lanes, Nabataean prosperity dwindled.

The sudden end of Madain Saleh has mystified a number

The exceptionally well-preserved tombs and dwellings at Madain Saleh give vivid evidence of the Nabataean civilization which flourished 2,000 years ago on the rich spice trade.

of scholars. There were no signs of battle and no evidence of disease. The tribe simply ceased to exist. The *Qur'an*, however, offers an explanation of how this branch of the Thamudians met its demise. *Surahs* 75-79 tell the story of the prophet Saleh who tried to return religious values to the decadent and materialistic Shamudians. They refused to accept Saleh as a messenger of Allah and arrogantly invited him to *bring about your threats* (*Surah* 77). In retribution, *the earthquake seized them and they lay dead, prostrate in their homes* (*Surah* 78).

Fortunately, their superb monuments survived, although they, too, inspire some unanswered questions. Where and how did the people live? Homes, palaces, and fortifications have yet to be found.

Virtually all of the 150 rock-carved tombs at Madain Saleh incorporate the same architectural style: a high doorway flanked by a pair of pilasters, traditional Nabataean capitals, and a main decoration of eagles (symbolic of force), urns (indicating a funerary nature), and a triangle containing an ugly mask, two serpents, and rosettas (representing the sun). These symbols were believed to protect the bodies.

One of the most interesting features of the imposing temple-like façades of the tombs is the small plaque carved above nearly all the doorways. The lengthy inscription in Nabaetean script gives the name of the owner of the tomb, names of relatives to be buried there, the date of the tomb's construction and, frequently, the name of the stonemason, as well as instructions on the use of the building and penalties against those who misuse it. In Petra, the northern stronghold of the Nabataeans, such inscriptions were the exception rather than the rule.

On average, each tomb took seven years to complete. Because craftsmen required a steady stream of water for the carving, they worked from the top of the rock formation downward. In order to dislodge large portions of rock, they chiselled cracks into which they placed sticks of wood. When the wood was burned it heated the fissure, at which time the craftsman poured in cold water to make the crack expand. Suitably placed cracks created convenient blocks of rock.

Tombs were closed with large wooden doorways. The spacious interiors held the remains of several generations of one family. Horizontal burial niches were carved in the walls as required. In a few well-used tombs, pits have been dug into the ground to accommodate the surplus of family members.

For those who could not afford majestic tombs, the top of a mammoth rock served as a temporary resting place. After the bodies decomposed in the open air, the bones were removed and buried.

In addition to tombs, there are many recesses cut into surrounding cliffs. These almost certainly had spiritual significance. One area, called the Sacred Way, was an important site of religious ceremonies and sacrificial offerings – both animal and human. At the entrance to the Sacred Way, worshippers stopped to pray: the imprints of hands still can be seen in the stone wall.

The only non-burial, non-religious site discovered so far is the Diwan Al-Sultan. Here the Nabataean kings would meet with followers and advisors.

Excavations continue under the watchful supervision of the Department of Antiquities. Visitors must obtain written permission from the Department to visit the area. Several check-points *en route* verify the validity of the papers. There are plans for an on-site museum and research centre where visitors and scholars will be able to learn more about an important but, so far, mysterious civilization.

In the meantime, modern man can only stand back in wonder at this monumental testimony to an ancient nation's skill, taste, and imagination – and an enthusiastic willingness and ability to meet the immense challenge imposed by nature.

MADINA. Madina, located 425 kilometres northeast of Jeddah and 447 kilometres north of Makkah, is the second holiest city in Islam. It was to Madina, or Yathrib as the city was called at the time, that the Prophet Muhammad and his followers fled in the year AD 622 to escape persecution in Makkah. Because of the willingness of the people of Madina to accept Muhammad, the city is also referred to as *Madina Al-Munawwarah*, The Enlightened City.

Madina and its environs have many Islamically important sites. The Prophet's Mosque, substantially enlarged over the centuries, was the original home and place of worship of Muhammad. It is here that the Prophet Muhammad and Abu Bakr and Omar, the first two Caliphs are buried. Al-Qiblatayn Mosque, meaning the mosque of the two *qiblas*, is so named because it was while praying in this mosque that God revealed to Muhammad that the orientation (*qibla*) during prayer should be towards Makkah rather than Jerusalem. Making a 180° turn, Muhammad complied with this instruction immediately. For that one period of worship, the mosque thus had two *qiblas*.

Only the airport and the Sheraton Hotel, both of which are situated on the outskirts of the city, are accessible to non-Muslims. *See also* HEJIRA CALENDAR.

MAHLAB. These chewy, rather bitter kernels come from black cherry trees. This is a popular Arabian ingredient for flavouring breads and pastries. *Mahlab* gives a pleasantly nutty taste.

MAJLIS. A *majlis*, an assembly of young and old male

relatives and friends, is a classic Arab tradition and Saudi Arabia's most basic form of government. The practice cuts across class and sectarian lines and preserves social cohesion. Ordinary citizens may petition the king and other officials directly and expect that appropriate action will be taken. The word *majlis* means 'the place of sitting', so *majlis* refers both to the room and to the function.

MAJLIS AS-SHURA. *See* CONSULTATIVE COUNCIL

MAKKAH (MECCA). This holiest city of Islam, located 70 kilometres east of Jeddah, was the birthplace of the Prophet Muhammad in AD 571 and the birthplace of Islam some 40 years later. Here, Prophet Muhammad received revelations from God and began his ministry.

Muslims refer to the city as *Makkah Al-Mukarramah*, Makkah the Revered, and as *Umm Al-Qura*, the Mother of all Villages. Five times each day, devout Muslims throughout the world face in the direction of Makkah to pray; at least once in their lives, health and finances permitting, it is the obligation of Muslims to make a pilgrimage to Makkah.

The area was first settled by Abraham, his wife Hagar, and their infant son Ishmael. Here, Hagar made the miraculous discovery of the life-saving water which came to be known as *Zamzam*. Here, God instructed Abraham to build the first house of worship, the holy *ka'ba*. Makkah has been a centre of pilgrimage for 5,000 years.

The focal point of the city is the Grand Mosque, an imposing structure which has been enlarged 10 times between 638 and 1995 to cope with increasing numbers of pilgrims. Within the mosque area are the *ka'ba* and the sacred *Zamzam* well.

With the exception of Aiyad Castle, the old Turkish fort, places of interest in the city are related to the history of Islam:

homes of the Prophet, his favourite wife, and various Caliphs, the Mountain of Light where Muhammad received his first revelation, and the Plain of Arafat where pilgrims gather for the most important day of the *hajj*.

With the steady influx of visitors came the exchange of ideas and opportunities for trading: pilgrims sell products from their home countries to help pay their travel expenses and they buy items related to the performance of their religious duties and souvenirs to take home. Makkah has prospered, both financially and culturally, as a result of all these exchanges.

Only Muslims are permitted to visit Makkah. Non-Muslims who are caught disobeying this restriction face fines and deportation. *See also* HAJJ; ISLAM; KA'BA; ZAMZAM WATER.

The beautiful Grand Mosque in Makkah seen in the glow of the setting sun.

MARRIAGE. Marriage brings much honour and joy to the Saudi family. When they marry, 'children' become adults.

Signature or oral ratification of the marriage contract legally sanctions the union. A judge (*qadhi*) conducts the ceremony. This official marriage normally takes place in the bride's home with the relatives of the bride and groom in attendance, although men remain segregated from the women. Even the bride and groom are in separate rooms and the *qadhi* goes from one to the other asking the groom and a representative of the bride if they accept each other. Once it has been established that there is no objection to the marriage, the paper work is attended to.

Consummation might take place on the day of the wedding or be delayed for days, weeks, or months. Nevertheless, the marriage is considered binding as soon as the contract has been signed. Even if the couple decides to dissolve the marriage before consummation, they must officially divorce.

In many rural areas, particularly among the bedouin, henna application becomes almost ritualistic on the night before a marriage (but only for the woman's first marriage). The female members of the wedding party gather together for the *lailat al hinna'* (night of henna) to have their hands and feet richly adorned. The bride wears pretty, embroidered bags over her hands to avoid staining her clothes. She keeps the bags as a wedding memento.

Men and women celebrate the marriage separately and in different ways. The men gather for a large dinner after *isha* prayer and leave early. The women's wedding party is a festive occasion with music, dancing, singing, food, beverages, and incense which continues into the small hours of the morning. The bride and groom arrive at the women's party around midnight. Seated on elevated chairs, the newlyweds accept the congratulations and good wishes of the guests.

Some wedding parties continue for four days but the groom appears with the bride only on the first night. Until recently, families held the parties at home. Now the functions more commonly occur in hotels or purpose-built wedding palaces.

After the celebration, the couple is escorted to their new home. The groom throws coins to the accompanying children and presents the adults with gifts. He gives his mother-in-law jewellery or cash in return for unveiling her face to him.

In the most traditional families, the wedding night is the first time that the couple is alone together. The bride often wears green as a sign of fertility. The following morning, the groom offers his wife a special gift (*subbhah*) of gold or jewellery to commemorate the occasion.

Because of the penchant for privacy, Saudis never publicize betrothals and marriages, even when the bride or groom is a prominent citizen. *See also* BETROTHAL; DIVORCE; MARRIAGE CONTRACT; WEDDING PALACE.

MARRIAGE CONTRACT. *Milkah* means 'to own'. It signifies the transfer of responsibility from the girl's family to her new husband.

When a woman accepts a marriage proposal, a premarital contract (*milkah*) is drawn up and witnessed by two competent adults. It stipulates the amount of the dowry (*mahr*) and, occasionally, other conditions, all of which must be adhered to. The terms must be recorded with a judge (*qadhi*) for them to be binding in the event of divorce. Once the contract has been signed and witnessed, the couple is legally married, although they don't usually consumate their marriage until after the wedding ceremony.

Shortly before the signing of the contract, the groom and his family present the bride-to-be with her dowry and other precious gifts. *See also* BETROTHAL; DIVORCE; MARRIAGE.

MISHLAH. *See* BISHT.

MISWAK. In cities, towns, and villages throughout the Kingdom, men can be seen sitting cross-legged on outstretched blankets with small bundles of pale brown sticks stacked neatly in front of them. These are not kindling or a mysterious kind of spice, as foreigners sometimes guess, but rather a hygienic tool called a *miswak*. For more than 1,000 years, Arabs have relied on the *miswak* to clean their teeth, freshen their breath, prevent plaque build-up, and stimulate the gums.

In Saudi Arabia the slightly bitter tasting *miswak* comes from the root of the arak tree (*Salvadora persica*). After soaking the *miswak* in water for several hours, one or two layers of the bark are pared off one end of the 20-centimetre long stick-like pieces to form bristles. Briefly chewing the exposed fibers softens the *miswak* sufficiently for brushing.

The *miswak* is used like a regular toothbrush; first massage the gums with the stick and then apply downward strokes on the upper teeth and upward strokes on the lower teeth, brushing both inner and outer surfaces. Remove worn fibers and expose new ones by further paring.

Scientific studies confirm the benefits of the *miswak*. Sinnegrin, tannic acid, and sodium carbonate in the root act as natural antiseptics. Other properties include anti-inflammatory substances, fluoride, and silicone which helps clean the teeth.

The *miswak* is commonly used during the holy month of Ramadan to freshen the mouth. Regular brushing during the day is not recommended during this period of fasting because of the risk of swallowing water.

MOSQUE. When the Prophet Muhammad settled in Madinah in AD 622, he built himself a simple mosque in which to worship. Through the centuries, mosques in Saudi Arabia have continued to be constructed in an undecorated, utilitarian style. The interior of mosques is devoid of furnishings or images depicting humans or animals. In accordance with Islam's teachings of equality, mosques have no places reserved for dignitaries.

The most important mosques in Islam are the immense Grand Mosque in Makkah and the Prophet's Mosque in Madina. They form the heart of the Muslim pilgrimage.

In Saudi Arabia non-Muslims, especially female non-Muslims, seldom enter mosques. Those who are invited should be circumspect in both dress and behaviour. *See also* HAJJ; ISLAM.

MOURNING. After burial, the three-day mourning period *(azza)* begins. If it is a man who has died, close male relatives go to the widow and other women of the family to announce the completion of the burial and to offer comfort. During this time the bereaved family receives condolences and is generally cared for by the community. Saudi men and women always receive condolences separately.

Close family members attend for the full three days. Verses from the *Qur'an* are read and visitors remember the good qualities of the deceased. Because it is prohibited to make a ritual of mourning, overt displays of grief should cease after three days. Although the tradition does not have its origins in Islam, some communities hold a remembrance celebration on the third, seventh, tenth, or fortieth day after death.

To ensure that she is not pregnant, a widow remains socially isolated for a period of four months and 10 days. A divorcée remains socially isolated for three complete menstrual cycles. During this period of *idda*, she receives no male visitors and minimizes attention to herself, including the wearing of jewellery and makeup.

If she is pregnant, her period of mourning extends to the time of childbirth. On the eve of the completion of mourning, the widow goes through a ritual cleansing, after which she may resume her normal activities. *See also* DEATH; BURIAL.

MUD HOUSE. *See* ARCHITECTURE.

MURABBA PALACE. In 1932, the same year he proclaimed the creation of the Kingdom of Saudi Arabia, King Abdul Aziz (Ibn Saud) established his seat of power in the newly constructed mud palace which he named Murabba (meaning 'square'). Originally situated on the fringe of Riyadh, the handsomely restored palace is now a museum and a focal point in the recently established King Abdul Aziz Historical Centre. The precinct includes the spectacular National Museum and the King Abdul Aziz Foundation for Research and Archives.

MUSEUMS. Most areas of historical/archaeological importance now have small but interesting museums. These are either purpose built or have been established as part of an existing building of historical interest. Following are brief descriptions of some of the museums in the main cities.

***Riyadh*.** **King Abdul Aziz Historical Centre** comprises the National Museum, the restored palace and mosque of King Abdul Aziz, the Darat Al-Malik Al-Abdul Aziz (a new institute and archive of the Al-Saud family), the water tower which was Riyadh's original landmark, a library, auditorium, and various restored mud buildings.

The emphasis at the Centre is on education, with displays clearly explained in both English and Arabic. The nine-acre site is located two kilometres north of Riyadh's original walled city. A central park contains 100 palm trees, planted to commemorate the *hejira* centennial of the Saudi state in 1999. The spectacular development is all the more remarkable because it was designed and constructed in only 27 months. During this brief period, the collections were gathered and the extensive displays created from scratch.

The National Museum houses a great many exhibits which together provide an overview of the dynamic changes in the life and culture of Arabia, covering the history from neolithic times, flora and fauna, the life of the Prophet and the spread of Islam.

King Faisal Centre for Research and Islamic Studies operates **The King Faisal Gallery** within the King Faisal Foundation building. The spacious, well-appointed museum is divided into three subject sections: pre-Islamic and Islamic

The National Museum in Riyadh.

history; the Kingdom during King Abdul Aziz's time, together with background information on the ruling Al-Saud family; and King Faisal, from his childhood until his death in 1975.

The innovative, hands-on **Science Oasis** in Riyadh's Diplomatic Quarter is a popular destination for children of all ages. With stimulating indoor and outdoor exhibits, children are taken from applied levels to the abstract.

Jeddah. The **Museum of Archaeology and Ethnography** has a wide-ranging collection of regional artefacts from the prehistoric to more recent times. Displays include calligraphy, local architecture, weapons and exhibits on King Abdul Aziz and the Zubaydah Road.

A restored 200-year-old former British Legation now houses Jeddah's **Municipality Museum**. Most of the exhibits are labeled only in Arabic. An appointment is necessary before visiting.

One of the most unusual museums in the entire Kingdom is the **Museum of Abdel Raouf Hasan Khalil.** More than 10,000 items are displayed in a pleasantly chaotic jumble in four buildings: House of Saudi Arabian Legacy, Islamic Legacy House, World Legacy, and General Legacy. The collections range from architecture to coins and from true treasures to tasteless curios.

Dhahran. The world-class **Aramco Oil Exhibit**, located near Aramco's Dhahran headquarters, is the Eastern Province's most famous museum. The high-tech displays, both static and hands-on, dramatically illustrate the story of Saudi Arabia's petroleum industry. The museum's centrepiece, reputedly the finest presentation of its kind, explains the contributions of medieval Muslim scientists to humanity. *See also* MURABBA PALACE; MUSMAK FORT.

MUSIC. The melodies of traditional songs tend to be simply structured and repeated throughout the song, the emphasis being placed on the words rather than the tune. Often, as in the *qasida*, the words of the songs come from narrative poetry. Song styles differ, depending on the location and the occasion. In the coastal areas, for example, the theme concerns the sea; in the Hijaz, the more cosmopolitan part of the Kingdom, memories of the Arab occupation in Andalusia exist in the local folk music called *al-sibha*; at wedding parties for women, women sing local folk songs. Each town and village has its own specific songs and music, although a number of musical aspects and some themes may be shared.

A pulsating beat is an important feature of Arab music.

At a men's social, musicians provide entertainment.

This is accomplished by musical instruments, particularly drums, and/or by rhythmic clapping.

MUSICAL INSTRUMENT. Singers and dancers are always accompanied by one or more types of drums. These include the *tar* (a frame drum), the *zir ardhi* (a shallow drum made of clay), the *tubul* (also made of clay but cylindrical in shape), the *zalafa* (multihandled), and the somewhat unconventional *tanaka* which is nothing more elaborate than a large olive or date tin with strategically punched holes, The *tanaka* is especially popular in southern Saudi Arabia. Instruments such as the *daff* (tambourine) and the *oud* (a fretless stringed instrument) are often added to the repertoire. The oboe-like woodwind instrument called the *mizmar* is frequently used in the Hijaz.

Many of the locally popular musicians are self-taught or have learned techniques from other family members.

MUSMAK FORT. In 1891 the rival Al-Rasheed dynasty from Hail wrested sovereignty over Najd from the Al-Sauds. By 1902 the young Abdul Aziz had planned an audacious strategy that would seal the fate of the Al-Sauds – one way or another.

Under cover of darkness and with only a handful of scouts, Abdul Aziz crept into the town of Riyadh and made his way to the home of an Al-Saud ally. After an informative briefing, the small band set out on their dangerous mission. They managed to gain access to the governor's house immediately across from the gates of the Musmak Fort. Abdul Aziz then sent for the less than three dozen reinforcements who had remained beyond sight of the fort. They, too, arrived safely and spent the rest of the night waiting for the appearance of Governor Ajlan. As a security measure, Ajlan slept within the confines of the fortress, exiting only at dawn to take breakfast with his wife and exercise his horses.

The beautifully restored Musmak Fort.

M

No sooner had the unsuspecting Ajlan and a few guards left the fort than Abdul Aziz gave the battle cry. The struggle was tense. Much more than lives hung in the balance. Suddenly, with victory or defeat only a breath away, Ajlan was killed. The amazingly successful surprise attack took only 20 minutes to force the submission of the fort. The garrison surrendered and the citizens swore allegiance to Abdul Aziz. The successful outcome of the bold raid returned to the Al-Sauds their honour and their possessions and provided the stronghold from which Abdul Aziz began his rule, planned the consolidation of the country's tribes and made further conquests.

Musmak Fort was originally constructed in 1865. It has now been converted into a museum. The rooms contain information and artefacts pertinent to the period of the conquest. Video films reenact the taking of the fort. Of special interest are the men's and women's *majlis* (sitting room) and the main gate. Each *majlis* has a special area for the making of coffee and tea and the storage of the related implements. The plaster-finished walls in the women's *majlis* are beautifully engraved with a series of geometric patterns.

Embedded in the fort's main gate is the tip of a spear which legend has romantically proclaimed as the one which killed Governor Ajlan and secured victory for the Al-Sauds. In fact the tip belonged to the spear of Fahad bin Jalawi. He tried to kill Ajlan but missed. When the Governor escaped into the fort, Abdullah bin Jalawi forced his way into the garrison and succeeded in killing Ajlan.

MUTAWWAH. The religious guardians of moral standards are called *mutawwa*. They belong to an organisation called The Protection of Virtue and the Prevention of Vice. Conflicts frequently arise over what constitutes the official policy and what is correct behaviour according to an individual *mutawwa*. Numerous unsuspecting individuals are caught in the crossfire and brought to special *mutawwa* jails for offenses which include wearing lipstick or travelling in a car with a person of the opposite sex to whom they are not married. Release is usually dependent upon the accused party signing a paper swearing not to commit the same offense again. Women are not released until their husbands or sponsors collect them.

The Saudi government states that no arrests or even approaches by the *mutawwa* can be made unless a civil policeman is in attendance.

N

NAFUD. Almost 55,000 square kilometres of northern Saudi Arabia is swept with a vast expanse of desert called the Great Nafud. In the 19th century, the intrepid English traveller Lady Anne Blunt, made history by being one of the few Europeans to make a successful crossing of the hostile sands. Some of the longitudinal dunes are many kilometres long and as high as 90 metres.

The only settlement in the Nafud is Jubba, a small town 100 kilometres northwest of Hail. This is the site of Thamudite rock carvings which date from 3000 BC. *See also* DESERT.

NAJD. Although the word *najd* means 'plainland', the topography of this central portion of the Kingdom is, in fact, quite varied. In addition to the predominant sand and gravel desert, mountains as high as 500 metres rise above valleys, oases, *wadis*, and escarpments.

Improved irrigation in the already lush oases has increased agriculture, which has always been the Najd's prime industry. The largest dairies in the world are located in Al-Kharj, outside Riyadh.

The main cities within the region are Riyadh, the Kingdom's capital, Buraydah, Hail, Jabrin, and Unayzah.

NAJRAN. Far off the beaten track of modern travels, the oasis of Najran nestles quietly into the southwest corner of Saudi Arabia. Centuries ago, however, it was an important stage along the famous trade routes. Here the settled people of southern Arabia met the camel-breeding bedouin tribes of central Arabia to negotiate for caravans to carry the lucrative supplies of frankincense and myrrh to eager northern markets.

Just as Najran's water and greenery made the oasis an ideal site for settlement, its strategic position at the crossroads of the trade routes made it a frequent target for invasion. A text from 7 BC mentions that the town was conquered and annexed by the then ruling Sabaean king Karib Al-Watar. Carvings, paintings, ancient scripts, and symbols on stone offer further clues to Najran's sometimes turbulent history. Although a plethora of artefacts and ruins provides insights into the daily life of centuries past, Najran's full story remains incomplete; the fascinating relics inspire more questions than answers.

Today it is not camel-breeders and conquerors who converge on Najran but agricultural specialists. Under the auspices of the United Nations' Food and Agriculture Organization (FAO), Najran's National Centre for Horticulture Research and Development was established in 1981. Now in its fourth five-year phase, the project has enjoyed uninhibited success. Although the fertile Najran valley grows an extensive variety of crops, the Research Centre focuses its activities on citrus. Experts come from all over the world to learn from the Centre's experiences.

Despite the fact that Najran is blessed with more water than neighbouring areas, there is still need for careful husbandry. Where surface irrigation used to be the norm, the Centre has succeeded in converting farmers to the merits of drip irrigation. As an incentive, farmers are offered, free of charge, disease-free budded trees. More than 81 per cent of local farmers now cooperate in this scheme, resulting in valuable water conservation.

The impressive Wadi Najran Dam has had a major impact on the area's water controls. The dam's catchment area is 4,800 square kilometres. The cylindrically-arched dam wall can hold back 86 million cubic metres of water. At full capacity, the reservoir presents an area of approximately five square kilometres. By storing water in times of excess and releasing it in times of need, the dam prevents the erosion of valuable agricultural land, allows expanded cultivation, and eliminates the devastation caused by flash flooding.

Blissfully removed from the impersonal veneer of cities, the people of Najran have retained their easy-going charm and exceptional hospitality. Here the pace is relaxed and the spirit of community prevails. In dress, too, people from Najran display an individuality: many of the men still wear bandoliers and *jambias;* the women are less formally veiled than in other parts of the country.

One of Najran's most striking features is its architecture, a reflection of the influence of neighbouring Yemen. Throughout town and countryside, graceful mud structures rise from the lush landscape. Many of the older, multi-storeyed buildings served as fortifications. Others, used as family homes, are decorated with charming whitewashed crenellations at roof level. The interiors often have brightly painted geometric patterns on the walls, richly beamed ceilings and, occasionally, stained glass windows.

Achievements are not limited to the region's illustrious past. An active municipality has infused the people with civic pride and embarked on urban development with exemplary enthusiasm. New buildings, improved infrastructure, and an upgrading of education and medical facilities are ongoing.

Perhaps most impressive, though, is the sensitive attention paid to aesthetics. Shade trees line spacious avenues, beautiful flower beds brighten intersections, and public parks and fountains are generously included in plans.

One of the goals of the administration is to introduce tourism to the area. By international standards of 5-star hotels and glitzy, manicured resorts, Najran has a long way to go, but for the tourist looking for unspoiled beauty in a friendly, exotic atmosphere, this is a delightful destination. The terrain includes forests, a man-made lake, lush valleys crisscrossed by *wadis* (dry river beds), and rugged, granite mountains which open on the north onto the Empty Quarter (Rub Al-Khali), Saudi Arabia's formidable sandy desert. Throughout the area, discreetly placed facilities such as picnic tables, toilets, and playgrounds enhance the visitor's enjoyment.

Needless to say, Najran's past is a salient factor in tourism. At Al-Okhdood, Najran's most important archaeological site, a well laid out museum informs visitors about the various aspects of life in Najran from antiquity to recent times. Al-Okhdood is mentioned in the holy *Qur'an* as the site of the infamous massacre of Christians in AD 525. The large trench in which the captive population was burned can still be seen. Excavations will no doubt unearth exciting finds at this site and others still to be discovered.

In the old town of Abu Saoud, the beautifully restored governor's palace, dating from 1940, is a touristic jewel which now serves as a period museum. Nearby, the *suq* (market) sells a cornucopia of local crafts and produce. One part of the *suq* is dedicated to the sale of old and new swords, daggers, and guns. Prices are still reasonable for intricately worked silver-hilted weapons. Colourfully embroidered *jambia* belts can be adapted to make an original fashion accessory. More treasures are to be found in the antique *suq*.

Wooden bowls, bedouin jewellery, old coins, and other relics from yesteryear all make interesting souvenirs for which to bargain, sometimes over a cup of tea.

Najran's temperate climate makes it a pleasant destination throughout the year. Hopefully the delightful character of the Najranis will emerge intact from yet another invasion of their lovely oasis – this time by tourists.

NAME. Names indicate patrilineal descent. At birth, a child is given only one name of his or her own. This precedes the descriptor *ibn* or *bin* (son of) or *bint* (daughter of), followed by the father's name, another *ibn*, *bin*, or *bint* and the grandfather's name, and so on, normally not exceeding four generations. Although confusing to foreigners, the system quickly establishes descent within the large family groupings.

The style of family names indicates tribal origin. People from the south take their family names, such as Zahrani or Gahtani, from villages. People from the Hijaz, Saudi Arabia's western province, distinguish themselves with the use of three names only: the person's given name, the father's given name, and the grandfather's given name, as in 'Sarah/Muhammad Yusef Abdullah'. In the Hijaz only, a boy might be given the additional name of Muhammad or Ahmad before his chosen name. This is believed to bring extra blessings upon the child. In the north of the Kingdom, the tribal name is used without *Al* or *bin* preceding. Because of the history of later settlement and migration, tribes from the Eastern Province have no specific pattern to their names.

Saudi women always retain their own family name, even after marriage. To facilitate introductions in Western society, a wife is often referred to as Mrs. (husband's last name). It is accepted, however, to introduce her simply by her first name, without 'Mrs.': 'This is Sarah, the wife of Muhammad (last name)' or 'This is Muhammad and his wife Sarah.'

NATIONAL DAY. This is the only secular holiday officially celebrated in Saudi Arabia and the only holiday which falls on the same date each year in the Gregorian calendar: 23 September, corresponding to the first day of Libra in the zodiac calendar. It represents the anniversary of the unification of the Kingdom under King Abdul Aziz in 1932.

NEWSPAPER. Considering its relatively small population, Saudi Arabia has an impressive number of national newspapers. The *Arab News*, *Saudi Gazette*, and *Riyadh Daily* are published in English. There are eight Arabic-language newspapers, of which *Ar Riyadh* (published in Riyadh) and *Al Jazirah* (published in Jeddah) have the widest circulation.

Although there is no official prepublication censorship by the government, editors are careful not to print anything which may be perceived as politically or religiously unacceptable. Those editors who dare to cross the line are severely reprimanded and may even be dismissed. Foreign publications face heavy censorship by the Saudi Ministry of Information before being released for sale.

NUMBERS. Although Arabic script is read from right to left, numbers are read from left to right. The pattern is slightly complicated when there are hyphenated numbers. For

١	٢	٣	٤	٥	٦	٧	٨	٩	٠
1	2	3	4	5	6	7	8	9	0

example, in Arabic the numerals 123-456 would actually be read as 456-123. Each block of numbers before or after the hyphen is read as a total unit using a left-to-right sequence. '456' is read before '123' because it falls under the right-to-left rule used for script. A frequent confusion over telephone numbers illustrates this problem!

Non-Arabs tend to refer to numbers written in Arabic script as 'Arabic numbers'. In fact, the Arabs had no number system of their own; they first adopted and then, through the spread of Islam, disseminated the Hindu pure place value system. The use of decimals and zeros made it faster and easier to solve complex mathematical problems. Originally written in Sanskrit, the Hindi numbers were gradually modified to suit the Arabic script style. Western numerals are adapted from the Arabic style.

O

OASIS. Within the vast expanses of desert that make up so much of the land mass of Saudi Arabia, the country's many oases offer fertile reprieves from an otherwise unforgiving landscape.

Oases form when sufficient underground water makes its way to the surface to support vegetation on a permanent basis. Sometimes the water source is thousands of miles away from the oasis where it emerges. If the water supply ceases, shifting sands rapidly reclaim the area.

The cities, towns, and villages in Saudi Arabia's arid interior are formed around oases, including Riyadh, the Kingdom's capital. Al-Ahsa, in the Eastern

Al-Ahsa oasis seen from the air.

Province, is one of the largest oases in the world. *See also* AL-AHSA.

OIL. Saudi Arabia is the world's largest oil producer. It has approximately 26 per cent of the world's proven reserves of oil and the fourth largest reserves of natural gas. When people talk about the Saudi oil industry, it is inevitably in superlatives.

Although the Kingdom's discovery and commercial exploitation of this product is recent, oil has been familiar to Arabs for thousands of years. Clay tablets from the Mesopotamian region refer to crude oil as early as 2200 BC. Muslims used kerosene for heating and lighting more than 1,000 years before the technology reached Europe. In his monumental 15th century work *The All-Encompassing Dictionary* (*Al-Qamus Al-Muhit*), Abu Tahir Al-Fayruzabadi, one of the foremost scholars of his time, described the word *naft*, the Arabic for what we today refer to as petroleum: *The best grade of naphtha is the water-white* [kerosene]. *It is a good solvent, a dilutent, and an expectorant. Taken internally, it relieves cramps and aches of the belly and, when applied topically, it can sooth skin rashes and infections...The word naffatah has three meanings: a naphtha well or fountain, a naphtha lamp used for lighting, or the brass instrument used to throw naphtha.*

The discovery of oil in the Eastern Province in 1933 brought unimagined riches to a desert Kingdom which previously had suffered extreme poverty. King Abdul Aziz is known to have commented that he would have preferred if the geologists had found water instead of oil but he soon realised the value of the discovery. After months of tough negotiations with Standard Oil of California (Socal), King Abdul Aziz told his Finance Minister Abdullah Al-Sulaiman to *Put your trust in God and sign.* On 29 May 1933 Socal was granted exploration rights for a period of 60 years. The rest, as they say, is history. On 3 March 1938 oil gushed out of the well named Dammam Number 7 in commercially viable quantities. In 1940 an enormous field at Abqaiq was discovered. Three years later Bechtel began construction of the 50,000-barrels-per-day refinery at Ras Tanura.

The joint venture formed between Socal and Texaco created a company called Casoc. In 1944 this was renamed Arabian American Oil Company (Aramco). The addition of new shareholders (Exxon and Mobil) four years later led the way for rapid and substantial increases in productivity. By the 1980s, Aramco had become the largest oil exploration and development company in the world.

In order to bring oil from the eastern Arabian fields to the Mediterranean, work was begun on the Tapline (Trans-Arab pipeline), the most ambitious project ever undertaken by the oil

In 1938, at Dammam Number 7, the first Saudi oil was pumped to the surface.

industry and, at the time (1946), the largest privately financed construction project in the world.

In 1973, influenced by the ideological concerns of King Faisal, members of the Organisation of Arab Petroleum Exporting Countries (OAPEC) agreed to cut back production until Israeli forces withdrew from Jerusalem and the occupied lands. The subsequent prospect of the United States authorising more than $2 billion in military aid to Israel, as well as European and US support of Israel, decided OAPEC to embargo oil exports to the US and Europe. At the same time, they increased the barrel price from $1.77 to $3.05. It jumped again to $7 before the embargo was lifted two months later. Although King Faisal used oil as a weapon in the Arab-Israeli conflict for moral reasons, his actions brought Saudi Arabia and the other Arab oil-producing countries unprecedented wealth. Equally important, however, the gesture reminded OAPEC of its dependence on oil revenues from the west for its new-found affluence.

The 10-year period from 1975 is fondly remembered as the boom years. A seemingly limitless income allowed the country to surge forward in its development of a modern state. Everything was needed and nothing was too expensive, thanks to oil revenues.

Along with attending to the vital needs of infrastructure, the Saudi government has spent vast sums of money in trying to create industries which are independent of oil. This has been largely unsuccessful. Oil and oil by-products make up about 85 per cent of the country's exports, 90-95 per cent of export earnings, 70 per cent of its income, and almost 40 per cent of the GDP (gross domestic product). Asia is the Kingdom's largest market for oil and refined petroleum products, followed by the US, which takes 17 per cent of its crude oil imports from Saudi Arabia, and Europe.

Investment in support facilities for upstream and downstream aspects of the industry has been enormous. The industrial cities of Jubail, on the Gulf, and Yanbu, on the Red Sea, were created out of tiny fishing villages. These twin cities linked by a pipeline are home to the largest petrochemical industry in the world. In order to transport the oil, thousands of kilometres of pipeline have been laid; oil terminals, islands to accept tankers, and offshore separation plants have been built. By December 2000, 1,430 wells had been sunk in 77 oil and gas fields. More than 500 additional wells are planned to the end of 2002.

Giant flames of natural gas burning in the desert used to serve as beacons to the oil fields. This energy began to be harnessed in 1960 when Abqaiq became the site of the first gas plant, producing LPG (liquified petroleum gas) for export. Aramco is the world's largest producer of natural gas liquids, the necessary feedstock for the LPG and petrochemical industries.

In May 2001 Saudi Arabia awarded seven major international oil companies (ExxonMobil, Shell, BP, Phillips, Enron/Occidental, Total, and Conoco) the first of several contracts in the $25 billion natural gas projects called the Saudi Gas Initiative. These are the first new upstream contracts since nationalization in 1980. The Initiative is designed to integrate upstream gas development with downstream petrochemical industry. The enormous Ghawar field, located on the fringe of the Empty Quarter, accounts for one-third of the country's known gas reserves. The influx of capital in the form of offset programmes is an integral part of Saudi Arabia's current foreign investment strategy. *See also* JUBAIL; YANBU.

ORYX. Its exotic habitat and the fact that it was once so difficult to catch inspired imaginative minds to create fantastical stories about this graceful, hardy desert creature. No doubt it was the profile of the long, spiral horns of the *Oryx leucoryx*, appearing as a single horn protruding out of the antelope's forehead, which was the source of the unicorn legend. But long before this mythological creation, the oryx featured prominently in bedouin poetry as a symbol of strength and beauty.

The Arabian oryx travels in herds of 8-20 males and females. Males can weigh as much as 210 kilos. The

average shoulder height is 84 centimetres; length is approximately 165 centimetres. A male's horns can grow up to 75 centimetres. Spindly brown legs protrude from a silvery white body. The face has brown or black markings on the bridge of the long nose and the area between the horns.

Females give birth after a 260-day gestation period. They normally produce single births but, in conditions of plentiful food, twins are not unusual. Within hours of delivery, newborns are fit enough to travel with the herd.

Large hoofs enable the oryx to travel across the soft sand. Oryx use their feet to dig up plants and roots and to make depressions in the ground where they can lie down to release body heat and absorb the cooler temperatures through a 'thermal window', the light coat of hair on their bellies. A much denser covering of hair on the rest of the body effectively insulates against the sun.

Ideally suited for a harsh desert climate, the oryx can survive for years without water, obtaining enough moisture from dew and plants. This ability was vital when the relentless encroachment of man drove the oryx deeper into remote areas. They finally became restricted to the Nafud Desert and the Empty Quarter, some of the most hostile terrain on earth. Even this exile did not protect them from the ruthlessness of hunters with four-wheel drive vehicles and high powered rifles and machine guns. The animals became extinct in the wild in 1972. Successful breeding programmes of captured animals have resulted in the reintroduction of the oryx to the wild. The now protected species is thriving.

P

PERFUME. Exotic fragrances are an integral part of Saudi culture. The rose scents have been legendary for centuries, even in European literature: in an attempt to wash away her guilt, Lady Macbeth called for *the perfumes of Arabia.*

It is the unadulterated nature of Arabian perfume which makes it so popular – and expensive. The finest Saudi perfume, from the mountainous Taif area, contains only the oil from the region's fragrant rose petals. No alcohol or synthetic compounds are added. When the intense fragrance gets onto the clothes, the scent may even survive a washing. Needless to say, the concentrate should be applied sparingly.

Incense, too, is a type of ancient perfume. The fragrant smoke is wafted into the hair and clothing where the scent can linger for days. *See also* PERFUME PRODUCTION; INCENSE.

PERFUME PRODUCTION. In Saudi Arabia, the production of perfume occurs only in Taif and its environs, particularly the rural communities of Al-Hadda ('tranquility') and Al-Shafa ('the cure'). According to local opinion, the wild, oil-rich roses (*Rosa x Damascena trigintipetala)* which grow in the nearby Al-Hadda mountains make the best concentrate. Each manufacturer steadfastly believes that Taif's ideal climate and fine soil produce an unrivaled quality of perfume. They will not use other types of flowers, nor will they even use any roses other than those from Taif.

This conviction is so strong that the industry operates for only 40 days each year, in April/May, when the wild mountain roses bloom. While manufacturers in other countries import assorted petals in order to prolong the manufacturing period, Taif producers will not even consider the possibility, despite the fact that it would mean a more regular revenue.

The Arabic word *itr* means 'perfume' or 'essence'. From this has come the English 'attar' which has become synonymous with 'rose oil'. The English word 'perfume' derives from the Latin *perfumum*, meaning 'through smoke'. This is not an exact description of the process but certainly it bears a close enough resemblance. In fact, steam distillation produces the essential oils.

The roses are picked and delivered early in the morning, preferably before dawn, well before the sun rays and the heat of the day can damage the fragile petals. Once the flowers lose their freshness and start to turn brown, they become unsuitable for use. For this reason, most of the distillation plants are located near the farms. Manufacturers begin the process as soon as they receive the roses.

Ignoring this age of mechanization, all the procedures continue to be done by hand. Two kilos of flower heads are emptied into a large metal pot, most of which sits embedded in a concrete base. The processor then pours a bucket of water on top of the petals and gently presses them with his hands. This procedure is repeated until the pot is nearly full with approximately 50 kilos of petals. The metal pipe connects the pot to a considerably larger vat which holds 200 litres of cool water. A further metal pipe joins the vat to a 10-litre glass jug.

Gas heat is applied under the pot containing the petals until a temperature of 90-100ºC is reached. The processor frequently feels the pipe leading to the jug to make sure the pot is not getting too hot. Overheating results in burned or singed petals which spoil the smell and ruin the entire batch. Once the desired heat has been obtained, the temperature is allowed to drop to approximately 10ºC. The surrounding stone or concrete base helps maintain the optimal temperature. As manufacturer Al-Ghraibi notes, *It is long experience rather than scientific accuracy which ensures good batches.*

With correct temperature control, condensation gradually forms in the glass jars. It takes approximately 10 hours to fill the 10-litre jug on the first run. This yields mostly the valuable oil concentrate as well as a small amount of scented water which is sold as rose water. On the second run, which takes eight hours to fill 10 litres, the proportions are virtually reversed. The third and final run of seven hours produces rose water of lesser quality.

Although not nearly as valuable, the dramatically more affordable rose water enjoys a wide distribution in the Middle East. Primarily popular as a flavouring in food, it is also sprinkled on the hands and faces of guests at celebrations and consumed for medicinal purposes, particularly for heart and stomach problems. Good quality rose water (first cut only) can be distinguished from poorer grades (a blend of all three cuts) by shaking the bottle. The best water makes thousands of tiny air bubbles which remain suspended for as long as half a minute. Relatively few bubbles appear in lesser qualities.

Taif has no satellite industries from perfume, such as the making of colognes and bath oils. This would necessitate the addition of alcohol or other secondary substances to the essence. The Taif manufacturers prefer to keep their product pure, not even condoning blending. In sharp contrast, French perfumes normally contain only 10-15 per cent perfume concentrate.

Taif manufacturers have prominent customers from many

countries. There is obviously as much pride in wearing authenticity as there is in producing it. The tiny industry inspires a clinging to old values...and the achievement of perfection.

PETROGLYPH. Man has been using stone as his canvas for tens of thousands of years. Arabia's ancient art gallery can be found on rock surfaces throughout the peninsula. The main concentrations of Saudi Arabia's rock art is found in the north, south, and central regions, with the oldest carvings located in Jubba in the Nafud. Most of the sites are situated in what are now remote desert locations. Originally, thanks to once lush vegetation, these were areas of habitation. In addition, petroglyphs appeared along the famous trade routes, like permanent billboards.

Rock art is divided into petroglyphs (carved drawings and inscriptions) and paintings. Of the approximately 1,200 catalogued rock art sites in Saudi Arabia, only three or four paintings have survived the passage of time.

Ancient artists chose flat, relatively smooth surfaces on which they chiselled their pictographic communications. Although it is impossible to date petroglyphs accurately, approximate age is established based on artefacts found near

A group of onagers, or wild asses, are vividly depicted on this sandstone rock face.

the sites. The earliest rock art is distinguished by large human and animalistic forms. These works are impressive for the great skill with which they have been executed, particularly considering the crude instruments and the difficulty of accessing many of the surfaces. Through the millennia, the figures became smaller and, often, more abstract. Gradually, the art moved towards outline drawings and then to the stick figures which immediately preceded script.

Drawings throughout the ages represented religious and cultural ideas and events. Often these messages were superimposed upon older drawings. Gods and goddesses carved into rock faces served as open-air temples for nomadic tribes and passing travellers. Symbols indicating the location of water no doubt were read with relief by many itinerants. Animal figures far exceed those of humans or other forms. Hunting scenes reveal a bounty of animals that desert conditions have made extinct in the region. These include elephants, lions, and ostrich. Cattle, a frequently depicted animal, are portrayed not only as a domesticated and hunted animal but also as a sacred beast, often in a sacrificial context.

Carvings of tribal dances confirm that this tradition has remained virtually unchanged for more than 5,000 years. Although the bodies of men and woman are human-like, faces remain consistently ambiguous. An interesting difference between rock art in the north and that of southern Arabia is that northern petroglyphs emphasize males while the southern figures are female-dominated.

One of the mysteries of rock art throughout the world, from the mountains of China to the caves of France, is that none of the drawings or inscriptions represents plant life.

Scientists believe that the individuals responsible for rock carving held important roles in their societies. They had the weighty responsibility of interpreting the images of their gods. As well, they created the ideology of, or imposed their ideology on, their society.

PILLARS OF ISLAM. *See* FIVE PILLARS OF ISLAM.

POETRY. Poetry has a most respected place in Arab tradition. The poet was the chief spokesman for the tribe. He taught and entertained his people and immortalized their deeds with his words. At the same time, he was responsible for the spread of news and propaganda. While the Huns were ravaging Europe, Arabia held annual poetry competitions at gatherings such as the famous Suq Okaz outside Taif.

Three main themes run through pre-Islamic poetry: love, travel, and glorification of self and/or tribe and condemnation of enemies. During the early Islamic and Ummayad period (AD 622-750) poetry became less simple and pure and more complex and diverse with the evolution of a sophisticated, urban society. According to the historian Hitti, the *Oasidah*, an ode celebrating the heroes of Arabia's deserts, *surpasses the* Iliad *and the* Odyssey *in metrical complexity and elaboration.*

Most of the early poems were sung; this powerful rhythm cannot be imitated easily in other languages. Translations of modern poetry are somewhat more effective because greater emphasis is placed on content than on form. The stress is not on how the poem is recited but on what is said.

In addition to classical Arabic poetry, the vernacular Nabati poetry is extremely popular in Saudi Arabia. *See also* LITERATURE.

P

POPULATION. The country's first full census was taken in 1974. At that time the population was recorded as just over seven million, including 73,000 Saudis living abroad. Since the 1970s, living conditions have improved dramatically and Saudi Arabia has witnessed an annual growth rate in excess of 3 per cent. Today, more than 22 million people live in the Kingdom. Approximately 50 per cent is under the age of 16. Saudiization has attempted to reduce the country's dependency on foreigners but guest workers, mainly from India, Pakistan, and other Arab countries still account for 35 per cent of the population.

Because so much of Saudi Arabia is uninhabitable, there is an average of only nine people per square kilometre. In England, in comparison, the population density is 375 people per square kilometre. The vast majority of the population, 83 per cent lives in urban areas.

Only Muslims can become Saudi citizens. Sunnis comprise 90 per cent of the population. The minority Shi'ites live mainly in northeast Saudi Arabia.

The greatest ethnic diversity can be found on the west coast where centuries of trading activities brought travellers from all over the known world. The central region, traditionally more isolated, has a more homogeneous makeup.

POSTAGE STAMP. A limited postal system, provided by the Egyptians in Jeddah and then by the Turks throughout the Hijaz and over to towns on the Gulf, operated from the latter part of the 19th century until 1919 when the last Turkish post office closed. They used stamps issued by the governments of Egypt and Turkey.

The first specially produced postage stamps were introduced into what is now Saudi Arabia in 1916 on the occasion of the Hashemite Sharif Hussein declaring himself King of the Hijaz. Col. T.E. Lawrence (Lawrence of Arabia) helped to choose the calligraphic design.

After Abdul Aziz captured Jeddah in 1925, the existing stock of stamps was overprinted: 'Hijazi Postage', for example, was replaced with 'Najdi Postage'. The first official Saudi stamps, printed in Egypt and inscribed 'Hijaz and Najd', appeared in 1926.

The rarest Saudi stamps are those commemorating the naming of King Abdul Aziz's son Prince Saud as Crown Prince. These sets, issued in 1934, were the first with the inscription 'Saudi Arabia'.

POTTERY. Because so much of the population was nomadic, pottery was never an important craft in Saudi Arabia. Only in Hofuf, in the Eastern Province, did pottery prevail. This is principally due to the fact that the area has suitable clay and plenty of water. The red clay is mixed with sand. Nine generations of the same family have worked the potteries at Jebel Al-Qara outside Hofuf.

Hofuf pottery never reached a high level of sophistication. Most of the traditional work is unglazed. Plant pots, often with pointed bases that require metal stands for support, are among the most popular and locally distinctive items.

PRAYER CALL. Five times a day, devout Muslims turn toward Makkah and offer prayers in a prescribed manner. The time for each prayer (*salah*) is determined by the arrival of dawn, midday, and dusk. There is also a prayer in mid afternoon and one an hour after the dusk prayer.

Muezzins call the faithful to prayer by chanting the prayer *God is great* (*allahu akbar*), *God is great, I testify that there is no god but God; I testify that Muhammad is the Messenger of God; come to prayer; come to salvation; God is great; there is no god but God*. In former times, this was done without mechanical assistance; nowadays the *muezzins'* voices are carried with the aid of loudspeakers that have been installed in the minarets, the tall spires that rise above the roofs of the mosques. Each mosque has its own *muezzin*; in a town or city with many mosques, the resulting cacophony eclipses all other sounds. *See also* FIVE PILLARS OF ISLAM.

PROVINCE. There are 14 provinces or governorates within the borders of Saudi Arabia. Each is ruled by a governor or *emir*. Governors are appointed by the king and report to a central authority in Riyadh. The governor is responsible for his region's development. He controls all government bodies and public organisations within the province. *See also* individual listings.

Al-Baha. This southwestern region is located between Taif in the north and Asir in the south. It is the smallest of the Kingdom's provinces. The capital is the town of the same name.

Al-Jawf. Sakaka, the capital city of Al-Jawf, sits on the northern edge of the great Nafud desert. The region is famous for its olives.

Asir. Asir has distinguished itself as an area of progressive ideas. It was here that the Arabian peninsula's first national park was created; here that the Kingdom's venture into tourism had its beginnings. The Asir hosts more recreational visitors than any other destination in Saudi Arabia. Such a statistic is hardly surprising considering the rugged scenic beauty and the quiet pace of the rural life.

Eastern Province. This is the heart of Saudi Arabia's lucrative oil industry. The capital, Dammam, is part of a triangle of cities that have grown at a phenomenal rate, from sleepy fishing villages to busy cities, in only 60 years.

Hail. Hugging the southern border of the Nafud desert, Hail was once an important rest point on the famous caravan route. The Jabal Shammar mountains surround the fertile valley of Hail.

Jizan. The thatched *rondavel* homes in this coastal southwest province are reminders of African pilgrim traffic over the centuries. Jizan has the benefit of both beautiful land scenery and the marvels of the Red Sea.

Makkah (Mecca). This city and province of the same name is home to the holiest shrine in Islam, the *ka'ba.* Makkah was also the birthplace of the Prophet Muhammad. Millions of pilgrims descend on Makkah each year. Only Muslims are allowed within the precints of the city. The mountain city of Taif, called the summer capital, and Jeddah, the Kingdom's major commercial centre, are located in the province of Makkah.

Madina. This small emirate is the second holiest place in Islam. It was to Madina that the Prophet Muhammad fled to escape persecution. Non-Muslims are allowed in the outskirts of the city but not within the city itself.

Najran. The peaceful oasis town of Najran is the administrative centre of this province that includes great stretches of the dramatic Empty Quarter.

Northern Province. Arar, the capital of this remote region, is close to the Iraqi border. The Gulf War brought the area temporary prominence.

Qassim. Northwest of Riyadh is the beautifully fertile province of Qassim. Buraydah, the capital, is perhaps the most religiously austere place in the Kingdom.

Qurayat. This northern province is close to the Jordanian border.

Riyadh. As well as being the capital of the province by the same name, the city of Riyadh is the capital of the Kingdom of Saudi Arabia. It was from his base in Riyadh that Abdul Aziz unified the various tribes throughout the country.

Tabuk. This remote northwestern province and city by the same name is an important military base. The city of Tabuk is sometimes used as a starting point for trips to Jordan.

P

Q

QASSIM. When the great traveller Charles Doughty arrived in Qassim at the end of the 19th century, he commented, *We were now in Kasim, the populous (and religious) nefud country of the caravaners...the inhabitants are become as townsmen: their deep sand country, in the midst of high Arabia, is hardly less settled than Syria. The Kusman are prudent and adventurous.*

The lushness of this central province made it a welcome stopover on the often rigorous caravan routes. Almost completely surrounded by harsh desert, Qassim is a miracle of fertility. The country's first agricultural college was built in Buraydah, the region's principal city.

The great Wadi Rima, originating in the lava hills of Khaybar 650 kilometres west, flows through the province, eventually exhausting itself in the Dahna dunes on the southern edge of the Nafud. Although dry for much of the year, the occasional furious floods can be frightening. Wadi Rima provides the ground water within a wide radius of its banks. The Wadi separates Buraydah from its twin city Unayzah, 24 kilometres to the south. *See also* BURAYDAH; UNAYZAH.

QATIF. This city lies about 13 kilometres north of Dammam. With archaeological evidence dating back to 3500 BC, Qatif is one of the oldest settlements in this part of the Gulf. Unfortunately, many of its interesting old buildings have been demolished in recent times. Some early European maps refer to the Gulf as the 'Sea of Alcatif', supporting the claim of Qatif's former prominence.

QIBLA. This is the direction of the holy *ka'aba* in Makkah and the direction towards which all Muslims must face when they pray. Hotel rooms usually have a large printed arrow stuck onto a table pointing towards Makkah to assist guests who wish to pray.

QUR'AN. The *Qur'an* (meaning 'to recite' or 'to read aloud') is the holy book and the essence of Islam. Revealed to the Prophet Muhammad by God during a 23-year period, the *Qur'an* contains the complete and unequivocal guidelines of a Muslim's life.

The *surahs* (chapters) of the *Qur'an* were first committed to memory by Muhammad and his followers as they were received from God. Knowing that, over time, orally transmitted messages might be diluted or embellished, Muhammad instructed that the revelations should be written down according to his specific instructions concerning the arrangement of the verses and chapters. The resulting collation, the Holy *Qur'an*, was completed in AD 651. Each of the 114 *surahs* comprises several verses (*ayas*). With the exception of the first chapter which is very short, chapters of the *Qur'an* are arranged in order of decreasing length, not in the order in which they were revealed.

The faithfully reproduced text has remained unchanged for more than 1,400 years. No variations are permitted. Muslims around the world study the *Qur'an* in Arabic because they believe that this is the only way to keep the message pure. *See also* ISLAM.

R

RADIO. The Broadcasting Service of the Kingdom of Saudi Arabia (BSKSA) provides national shortwave, AM and FM services. Like television, radio got off to a rocky start when conservatives objected to its introduction on the grounds that it would corrupt followers and detract from the path of Islam. By initially broadcasting readings from the *Qur'an*, the late King Faisal showed that the government was prepared to ensure that this new technology would provide the people with good influences. Today, in addition to local and Aramco stations, international broadcasts, such as BBC World and VOA, can be picked up in the Kingdom. As of 1998, listeners could tune into 43 AM, 31 FM, and 2 shortwave stations.

RAILWAY. For such a large country, there are surprisingly few rail links. At present, the only line is the 480-kilometre stretch between Riyadh and Dammam, via Hofuf and Abqaiq. Work began on the project at the end of WWII with the help of Italian and Pakistani technicians. King Abdul Aziz opened the line on 2 October 1951.

The coaches are air-conditioned and have a restaurant car. First-class costs 60 riyals one way and second-class costs 40 riyals one way. Children under 12 travel at half fare. Morning and evening departures can be busy so it is best to buy tickets a day in advance. Ticket windows close during prayer times; passengers who leave ticket purchases to the last minute may find themselves out of luck if the departure time coincides with *salah*.

Muslim women who travel by train must be accompanied by their husband or *mehram* (male relatives whom they cannot marry). Non-Muslim women should have their husbands or a female friend with them.

The Ministry of Communications has confirmed that it is economically feasible to introduce lines in other parts of the country, particularly between Dammam and Jubail to service the petrochemical industry, and between Jeddah-Makkah-Madinah for the pilgrims. The World Bank has made strong recommendations for 2,469 kilometres of new track: east-west lines linking Jeddah port with ports in Dammam and Jubail, and north-south tracks between Riyadh, Qassim, Hail, and Al-Jawf. So far, no contracts have been awarded.

Consideration is being given to privatising the rail sector. The government is currently in discussion with international investors who have experience in this field. The expansion programme is aimed at improving service and completely modernising existing lines. One of the impediments to new development has been the difficulties in expropriating the necessary land. *See also* HIJAZ RAILWAY.

RAMADAN. Ramadan is the holiest month in Islam's *hejira* calendar. It was during Ramadan that God first began his 23 years of revelations to the Prophet Muhammad. In commemoration, Muslims devote the daylight hours of Ramadan to the regimen of fasting. This not only serves as exacting self-discipline but teaches through experience the deprivations of thirst and hunger. Throughout Ramadan, between dawn and dusk, Muslims abstain from food, drink, cigarettes, and sensual pleasures and devote themselves to more spiritual endeavours. The first light of dawn is generally accepted to occur when a white thread can be distinguished from a black one, approximately two hours before sunrise.

Despite the difficulties of fasting, Muslims are expected to maintain their normal routines. Those who use Ramadan as an excuse to shirk work and other responsibilities effectively break their fast. Besides physical abstention, Muslims must refrain from losing control of their temper and their speech. Anyone who breaks the fast must make up the days before the next Ramadan or feed one poor person for each fasting day missed. Exemptions from fasting are granted to pregnant, nursing, or menstruating women, the old or infirm, young children, the insane, and people travelling further than 80 kilometres.

Traditionally, the fast is broken after the sunset prayer with a light snack, often fresh dates and water. A more substantial meal is taken after the fifth prayer (*isha*), usually about 1 1/2 hours after dusk.

During Ramadan, spiritual and social awareness increase. Muslims pray more, especially at night, spend more time in studying the *Qur'an*, and perform more acts of charity. This unity of worship and sharing reinforces the spirit of brotherhood.

Ramadan 27, *Lailat Al-Qadr* (night of power and greatness), the night before the last night of Ramadan, is considered to be the most holy time in the holiest month and is a period of increased religious activity. It commemorates the approximate time when Muhammad received his first revelations. The faithful believe that prayers of petition made on this night will be answered.

In deference to people who are fasting, non-Muslims should refrain from eating, drinking or smoking in public during the day throughout the month of Ramadan. Both dress and behaviour should be particularly circumspect during this period.

RAMADAN FOOD. Paradoxically, it is during this holy month of fasting from dawn to dusk when the greatest variety of traditional foods appears. This time of spiritual renewal and of reestablishing the close bonds of family inspires an unprecedented flurry of cooking and eating. Many of the foods are prepared only during Ramadan.

The Ramadan fast is broken after the sunset *iftar* prayer with easily digestible dates and Arabic coffee. This light 'break-fast' may be followed by a thick soup, cheese and meat pastries called *sambouseks*, a spaghetti topped with a sauce made from yoghurt, garlic, mint, and black pepper, and *foul* (beans). In order to sustain energy, sweets are an important part of the meal. These include such favourites as *muhalabiya, konaffa, gatiyif, crème caramel,* and custard.

These foods are washed down with *gamaradeen* (apricot juice), orange juice, or the slightly salty tasting water of the 4,000 year old well of Zamzam in Makkah. *Subya* is also popular. It is a nutritious mixture of sugar, warm water, barley, cinnamon, cardamom, and yeast and is known to aid the digestive process.

The 0200h meal of *suhoor* is a more lavish event to which guests are usually invited. At this time Saudis traditionally eat *kapsa* (lamb and rice), yoghurt, *laban,* and salad. They drink tomato juice, tea, and plenty of water.

All eating and drinking must be completed before *imsak*, approximately 15 minutes before the call to dawn prayer. *See also* FOOD.

RAS TANURA. Only in existence since the post-war expansion of the oil industry, this port located 15 miles north of

Dammam has become one of the largest oil storage and shipping centres in the world. Because of the notoriously shallow coastal waters of the Arabian Gulf, long moles had to be constructed to enable access to seagoing tankers.

RED SEA. Many fascinating and frightening forms of a rich marine biology live in the exciting underwater paradise of the Red Sea, including important, undisturbed coral reefs. This 1,800-kilometre stretch of coastline has virtually no natural harbours. A portion of the magnificent seascape of the Red Sea and its beaches in the southwest is under the protection and supervision of Asir National Park. The Saudi government

The main refinery at Ras Tanura.

R

recognises its ecological responsibility to protect this fragile ecosystem and forbids the discharge of pollutants within 160 kilometres of the Saudi coastline. Control of litter and building rubble is more difficult and, in many areas, much less successful.

As well as being one of the world's best dive destinations, the Red Sea is a generous food source. Local fishermen still use the ancient hook-and-line method to catch the rich variety of fish for which the Red Sea is famous.

This body of water is also an important source of household and industrial water for the city of Jeddah. Desalination plants work constantly to provide a high standard of drinking water. Untreated salt water is necessary for the oil refineries, petrochemical factories, and cement plants along the coast. *See also* FARASAN ISLANDS

RIYADH. Considering that at the turn of the 20th century there were no main roads leading to Riyadh, this desert capital has come a long way. King Abdul Aziz's seat of government was only 2.5 square kilometres in 1932. Seventy years later it had expanded to over 1,600 square kilometres, more than 400 times the size of the enclave Abdul Aziz captured in 1902.

Until the 12th century, Riyadh was called Hajr. The word 'riyadh' means 'gardens'. The description referred to the many palm groves in the large oasis. Beyond the plantations, however, vegetation was sparse. Today, improved water supplies allow the luxury of lawns and exotic gardens, making the name 'riyadh' particularly appropriate.

Although Riyadh has always been the base of the ruling Al-Sauds, it was only in the 1970s that ministries and embassies relocated from the more cosmopolitan city of Jeddah to the traditional capital of Riyadh. Situated in the heart of the harsh lands of the Arabian peninsula, Riyadh's geographical disadvantage in former times also isolated the area culturally. A dearth of outside influences meant that both the city and the region of the same name remained a bastion of religious conservativism and puritan reformation.

With the exception of the few preserved mud structures, much of Riyadh has been constructed since the boom years of the 1970s. In a frenetic rush to the future, symbols of the past were too often razed or abandoned and replaced with inferior concrete substitutes. Architecture ranges from the nondescript to the exceptional, with a number of internationally acclaimed architects putting their signature to some of the city's finest buildings. Al-Faisaliah won the race to beome Riyadh's first skyscraper. The Kingdom project was the next to make its mark on the city skyline, exceeding Al-Faisaliah's 267 metres by a few metres. Undoubtedly, other mega constructions will soon follow.

The Ministry of the Interior building in Riyadh, looking like a giant space ship.

Riyadh is one of the fastest growing cities in the world. It long ago seeped beyond the confines of the thick, 7.5 metre tall mud wall which once surrounded the city. New suburbs to accommodate the rapidly increasing population of 3.5 million appear so quickly that construction is often completed before services such as water and electricity can catch up. The narrow streets of the past have been replaced by wide avenues and superhighways. Newcomers find it particularly difficult to get their bearings in this sprawling metropolis because most of the main street signs are in Arabic only and many streets have no names. Navigation is by landmarks.

ROCK ART. *See* PETROGLYPHS.

ROSE WATER. Gently scented rose water is a by-product of the perfume industry. The best grade of rose water comes from the first run in perfume production. The more common, less expensive commercial grades are a blend of three runs. These are most frequently used as a subtle flavouring in beverages and desserts. Rose water is reputed to be beneficial for the heart and stomach. *See also* PERFUME PRODUCTION.

ROYAL DIWAN. The king's executive office, his private office, and the offices of his principal advisers and heads of several government departments are located in the Royal Diwan. Here the routine business of running the country is conducted. Here, too, the king holds his regular *majlis*, where he receives petitions from his subjects.

ROYAL FAMILY. Saudi Arabia's ruling Al-Saud dynasty is descended from the Anizah tribal confederation. In varying degrees, the Al-Sauds have exerted their influence since the 1500s when they took control of Dir'iyyah, an oasis on the outskirts of modern-day Riyadh. Their rule remained local and relatively unimportant until the mid-1700s. At that time

Muhammad ibn Abdul Aziz Al-Saud made an historic military-religious alliance with the conservative reformer Muhammad ibn Abdul Wahhab. In exchange for Muhammed Al-Saud promising to rule according to the tenets of Islam, Abdul Wahhab agreed to give public support to the Al-Saud leadership. By the early 1800s, the Al-Sauds controlled Makkah and Madina in the west, the central Najd region, and much of the peninsula's east coast. The Ottomans brought an abrupt halt to their spread of power in 1818 with the capture and destruction of Dir'iyyah and the execution of the Al-Saud leader. The Al-Sauds regained control a few years later and moved their capital to Riyadh. The conquest of the rival Al-Rashid tribe sent the Al-Sauds into exile in Kuwait.

The current dynasty was founded by the charismatic Abdul Aziz ibn Saud (also known as Ibn Saud in the west). He successfully subdued the Al-Rashids at Riyadh's Musmak Fort in 1902. From this base over a 25-year period he achieved what no man before him had ever done: the unification of Arabian tribes. He consolidated his rule with the help of his sons and other direct descendants of the family patriarch Muhammed Al-Saud, particularly the patrilineal descendants of Abdul Aziz's grandfather Faisal ibn Turki. In 1932 Abdul Aziz proclaimed the territories under his control the Kingdom of Saudi Arabia.

Within the Al-Saud there are five principal clans: Al-Sudairi, Al-Thunayyan, Al-Jiluwi, Al-Al Shaikh and Al-Kabir. These are influential families into which the Al-Saud frequently marry.

Only sons and daughters directly descended from kings on the father's side can use the title HRH (His/Her Royal Highness). Other royals use the title HH (His/Her Highness).

So far, there have been five kings: Abd Al-Aziz Al-Saud (1926-1953), the founding father, and four of his sons: King

Saud (1953-1964), King Faisal (1964-1975), King Khaled (1975-1982), and King Fahd (1982-). HRH Prince Abdullah bin Abdul Aziz is Crown Prince, Deputy Prime Minister, and Commander of the National Guard; HRH Prince Sultan bin Abdul Aziz is Second Deputy Prime Minister and Minister of Defense and Aviation. *See also* MUSMAK FORT.

RUB AL-KHALI. *See* EMPTY QUARTER.

S

SALUKI. It is hard to imagine that the elegant saluki is more at home exercising his strong hunting instincts in the deserts of Arabia than appearing in show rings around the world. This sleek animal is one of the oldest breeds of dog. It is considered the progenitor of the greyhound, a larger variation of the species. Images of the saluki are recorded in the tombs of Egyptian pharaohs.

The name 'saluki' derives from Saluq, an area in Yemen from where the dogs are said to have originated.

Salukis are sight hounds (they use their highly developed vision to hunt), although they are also renowned for their uncanny sense of hearing. Well-trained salukis rarely lose their prey once it is sighted. The low-set heels of the hind legs were bred into the saluki to give added leverage for galloping and jumping in rough desert terrain.

The male saluki averages 58-71 centimetres in height; the female is slightly smaller. The silky coat of salukis may be either smooth or have feathered ears and tail.

The dog's great capacity for speed enables it to keep pace with the Arabian horses, making it invaluable when hunting gazelle. The saluki's sandy colour serves as excellent camouflage in its native desert environment where the quarry rarely recognizes the danger until it is too late. Owners need to give salukis plenty of exercise and ensure that the dogs are kept under control in rural areas where their strong hunting instincts may bring them in conflict with local farmers.

The remarkably intelligent saluki makes an excellent companion and a superb guard dog, yet it is gentle enough to be reliable around children. Odour-free, the saluki has the distinction of being one of only two breeds which the Arabs recognize as purebred and clean.

SANDALS. European-style shoes have crept into Saudi wardrobes but even the most urbane members of the population keep leather sandals *(na'al)* on hand. The traditional styles usually have colourful, geometric patterns painted on or sewn into the upper parts. In addition to a broad strip of leather across the foot, the large toe is covered. International manufacturers have bowed to market demands and produce chic footwear which is reminiscent of local custom while at the same time is an expression of modern tastes.

SAND DUNE. Sand dunes are sculptures on the canvas of the Kingdom's deserts. These wind-formed collections of loose, fine- and medium-grained (0.06-0.5mm) sand form domes, ripples, and ridges as a result of meeting obstructions in the terrain. Complex megadomes can be as wide as eight kilometres and as high as 150 metres. Occasionally, vegetation stabilizes dunes but more often the wind regularly alters their shape and size. Sometimes they make a substantial shift in position and other times it is only the lighter surface particles which gentle winds gather and redistribute. Solitary dunes have been moulded by multi-directional winds over a period of thousands of years. Many dunes are solid enough to support 4-wheel drive vehicles, although the skill of the driver will make the difference between successfully reaching the sumit and getting stuck along the way.

SESAME SEED. Sesame seeds are believed to be the oldest plant grown for oil. The seeds are used extensively in Middle Eastern cooking, either whole to decorate and flavour breads, pastry, and confectionary, or ground into a paste called *tahina*, an important ingredient in making *hummos*. The nutty flavour of the seeds is brought out with dry roasting. Sesame seeds and oil are mildly laxative.

SHAIKH. This title (pronounced 'shake'; often *mis*pronounced as 'sheek'), derives from the Arabic word *shaikhoukha*, meaning 'old age'. It is most usually given to the leader of a tribe or to a man who has earned stature in the community (and presumably has gained valuable experience along the way). For example, the heads of large trading establishments are usually referred to as 'shaikh' before their first name. Because the title denotes respect, it is sometimes used as a polite form of address or to refer to the revered head of a family.

In tribal societies, the honour of the title is bestowed not necessarily on the eldest member of the tribe but on the person who has shown wise leadership and decision-making capabilities. In former times, courage in battle was also an essential quality. A *Shaikh* is expected to be generous with his wealth and understanding of the problems of his 'family'. It is incumbent upon the *shaikh* to earn the allegiance of his people.

The stature of the *shaikh* depends on the strength of his tribe. The leader of a confederation of tribes, for example, is more powerful than the *shaikh* of a smaller, and therefore weaker, subtribe.

SHAMAGH. This red-and-white check head covering is worn by Saudi men. In the interior and rural parts of the peninsula, the checked style is preferred to the plain white fabric which is favoured in urban areas. The *shamagh* serves as both a protection from the sun and as a convenient nose and mouth cover in sand storms.

The large square of cotton or cotton blend is folded diagonally with the three points falling on each shoulder and down the back. It sits on top of the *taqiyah* (skull cap). Most men leave the *ghutra* or *shamagh* on at all times, except when relaxing at home. It is impolite to ask a Saudi to remove his head covering. *See also* DRESS; GHUTRAH.

SHAMAAL. These sand-laden winds originate in the Arabia's northern deserts. Travelling as fast as 50 kilometres/hour, a *shamaal* (pronounced sha-moll and meaning 'north') will often appear suddenly with little warning; other times there can be the scent of dust in the air for two or three days before the winds arrive. *Shamaals* are most prevalent in early summer, sometimes lasting several days at a time. The bedouin protect themselves from the blowing sand and dust by wrapping their *ghutra* or *shamagh* around the mouth and nose. Sand storms can be particularly uncomfortable for people who wear contact lenses.

SHARIA. *Sharia*, the legal framework of Islam, derives primarily from two sources: the *Qur'an*, Islam's holy book comprising God's revelations to the Prophet Muhammad, and the *sunnah*, examples of Muhammad's deeds and approvals concerning social matters. Secondary sources are *ijma*, a consensus of religious scholars, and *qiya*, which calls on interpretation based on precedence. Situations not covered in the *Qur'an* are called 'regulations', such as Labour Regulations.

Sharia is not secular, but ethical. Crimes are thus committed against the will of God – an unthinkable act. This, more than the harsh punishments, explains the Kingdom's low crime rate.

Saudi Arabia follows the Hanbali school of law. It strongly emphasizes the four acknowledged sources of reference and does not allow liberal influences.

As an integral part of Islam, *Sharia* embraces all aspects of communal and individual behaviour. In protecting the social order, *Sharia* places the rights of society over the rights of individuals, who are viewed as parts of the whole. Those who violate the peace and security of the community risk punishment proportional to the magnitude of the crime.

Although the code seems alien and harsh to the uninformed, in fact it has much in common with most systems practised in the West. The accused remains innocent until proven guilty or until he offers a confession of guilt. The onus of proof rests with the accuser who must provide a minimum of two eyewitnesses to the crime. Alternatively, the accuser may demand an oath of innocence from the defendant. In both civil and criminal proceedings a *qadhi* acts as judge and jury. The defendant has the right to appeal the *qadhi*'s decision. Legal costs are not recoverable. Non-religious courts are referred to as 'committees'.

Sentencing usually takes place without undue delay. Prison terms include the time served before the trial. Imprisonment is not only the result of conviction but may occur during investigations and until settlement of seemingly minor disputes.

Death sentences are carried out swiftly. In the case of murder, punishment may be determined by the victim's family rather than by the court. Sometimes the convicted person must wait for the victim's children to come of age and decide whether they want the accused to die or whether they will accept blood money in compensation.

Murderers and rapists suffer public decapitation; adulterers face death by stoning. Repeated theft is punishable by amputation of the right hand, although thieves who steal out of hunger or real need are let go; only crimes of greed are punishable. For these more serious offenses, the sentence must pass the high courts and receive final approval of the king before being carried out. Less severe penalties include public floggings, jail terms, fines, and deportation for non-Saudis. A flogging is intended to be more injurious to the pride than to the body.

SHAWARMA. The Saudi equivalent of fast food is the tasty and convenient *shawarma*. Thin slices of lamb or chicken are carved from huge hunks of pressed meat that turns on a vertical spit and is cooked with electric heat from behind. The meat is served in Arab flat bread that has been curled into a cone shape. Sauces such as yoghurt, garlic sauce, or chili sauce and a few chopped onions and tomatoes complete the inexpensive meal. *See also* FOOD.

SHAYLA. *See* TARHA.

SHEEP. Bedouin tribes divided themselves between those who herded camels and those who herded sheep. Of the two, camels were the more prestigious stock. The decline of the camel's usefulness with the advent of motorized vehicles, however, has given new importance to the sheep. The faster breeding rate of sheep combined with a substantially increased demand for mutton means a faster return on investment. This is an important consideration in modern times when the bedouin now have untraditional expenses such as trucks to buy and maintain.

Sheep cannot travel great distances in search of water and pastures. Overgrazing was therefore an unfortunate by-product of their survival. Not so long ago, it was common to see small herds of sheep grazing in empty urban lots. Now, they are often penned in huge areas on the outskirts of cities, convenient to market. They feed off fodder that is brought to them by truck.

The long-earred, long-haired local sheep are sometimes difficult to distinguish from the long-earred, long-haired goats. Only the tail, raised like a flag, on the goat differs from a sheep's tail which is always lowered.

No Saudi menu would be complete without a dish of mutton in one form or another. In Saudi Arabia, the fat-tailed, white fleeced *nami* sheep is considered the most flavourful of the breeds and is the most expensive. It originally came from Iraq.

SHISHA. Although health awareness programmes are beginning to erode the deep-rooted habit of cigarette smoking, the attraction of the ancient water pipe is increasing in popularity. This tall, elegant smoking apparatus is frequently referred to as a hubble-bubble or hubbly-bubbly because of the sound the water makes as it filters into a water-filled base. It is also referred to as a *narghile* in Arabic, meaning 'coconut'. In former times, the cooling water was kept in a coconut shell.

The tobacco mixture, flavoured with fruit or a herb and honey blend, sits in a clay bowl at the top of the *shisha* (pronounced 'sheesha', from the Persian for the glass water holder) and is covered in glowing charcoal embers. A glass bowl contains the water which cools the smoke. Two tubes extend from the glass bowl: a rigid one leading to the pipe bowl that holds the tobacco and a long, flexible one tipped with a filter/nozzle from which the smoker tranquilly inhales.

The *shisha* is decidedly less portable than a pack of cigarettes; *shisha* smokers therefore tend to gather at cafés dedicated to this socially amenable activity and spend several hours at a time puffing contentedly. These public cafés are exclusively for men, but it is acceptable for women to smoke the *shisha*.

Although *shisha* smoking is not associated with cancer, the long, deep breaths required to smoke the pipe can cause emphysema. Users should be aware that germs come not just from the nozzles (most regulars have their own nozzles and cafés provide clean nozzles for customers) but moreso from the tubes themselves which cannot be disinfected. Only if the *shisha* is used exclusively by the same person can the risk of respiratory infections be prevented.

SIRWAAL. These lightweight white shorts or long, drawstring pantaloons are worn under the *thobe*. *See also* DRESS.

S

SOUQ. *See* SUQ.

SPICE. Most historians agree that the Arabs, in their extensive search for a greater cross-section of pungent products, first introduced the highly esteemed spices of cinnamon and cassia to the Middle East in at least 2000 BC. Cardamom, ginger, turmeric, and others soon followed and quickly became favoured items of exchange.

Ever shrewd traders, the Arabs artfully withheld their source of supply from both curious buyers and potential competitors by inventing frightening tales which stressed the dangers they encountered in obtaining the spices. Cassia, according to their fantasies, grew in shallow lakes guarded by winged animals, while cinnamon could be found only in deep glens infested with poisonous snakes. Such imaginative narratives, of course, also served to enhance the prices of the goods. *See also* BAHARAT; CARDAMOM; LOOMI; MAHLAB; SESAME SEED; SUMAC; ZATAR.

SUMAC. This pleasantly sour and astringent spice is extremely popular in the Middle East. It is sprinkled on fish, meat, or poultry, added to salads or raw onions, used in stuffing for chicken, or mixed with yoghurt.

SUQ. The ancient precursors to shopping malls can still be found in lively abundance throughout Arabia. The most traditional of these numerous little hole-in-the-wall shops generally face onto dirt alleyways. Modern *suqs* (pronouned

Copper and brass items on sale in the antique suq in Riyadh.

'sooks') are warren-like, concrete shopping centres. These bustling markets sell everything from camels to clothes to jewellery. The exotic sights, sounds, and smells transport visitors to the past.

Some vendors may sit patiently behind their jumble of wares while others shout prices and entice customers. Cups of sweet tea may be offered to long-standing customers or those who look like potential buyers. In some shops, the goods may be laid out in an orderly fashion; in others, the best treasures are found by digging through heaps of dusty, often unrecognizable items.

Suqs, being the traditional central commercial area, also have assorted craftsmen. A sudden bright flare from a blow torch might reveal a wizened old man attaching decorative silver beads onto the hilt of a dagger.

In most towns, there is a weekly open-air market where people from outlying areas gather to purchase supplies and sell their produce. Some of the major markets are held only once a year. These attract the deep-desert bedouin tribes as well as sedentary communities. At these large gatherings, the buying and selling of livestock is as prominent as the more usual *suq* items.

In most *suqs* it is standard procedure to bargain. *See also* BARGAINING.

SUQ OKAZ. Just outside Taif, are the ruins of one of history's oldest *suqs* and, in its time, the most renowned in the Arab world. Traders from throughout the region took advantage of the large gathering to sell their commodities. Not only did *Suq Okaz* display a virtually unrivaled selection of goods but it was also the prime cultural gathering place for poetry readings. Major poets travelled great distances to participate in the annual competitions. The *suq* also served social and commercial purposes. Banners of Honour recognized the worthy and Banners of Treachery assailed the unworthy. It was an ideal setting to arrange marriages.

Political-religious problems finally caused the destruction of the *suq* in AD 754. Only a few stubborn walls and some graceful archways survive to remind us of the once lively marketplace.

T

TABUK. Tabuk (pronounced 'ta-book') is the closest Saudi city to the Jordanian border and is situated only 450 kilometres south of Amman and just a short drive to Petra. The province by the same name is the most populous of the Kingdom's remote northern governorates. It supports a strong military presence.

In history, the region of Tabuk was considered important enough by the mighty Babylonians that, for a brief period, they ruled their empire from the town of Taima. In more recent times, Tabuk city was the largest station on the ill-fated Hijaz railway. The extensively restored station complex includes the main station, barracks for Turkish soldiers, and an engine maintenance shed. Also of interest is the Tabuk Fort. In the mid 17th century, the Ottomans built the existing fort on the site of a 10th century fort. Permits are required from the Department of Antiquities in Riyadh in order to visit the historical sites.

The recent discovery of millions of tons of silica sand in a 40-kilometre stretch of northern Tabuk will support many of the Kingdom's downstream industries, including the manufacture of computer chips, contact lenses, and fiberglass. Mining exploitation will bring development and employment to this region.

TAIF. Taif had its beginnings as a city as far back as 670 BC and enjoyed the prestige of a commercially strategic centre for more than 1,000 years.

The two main ancient trade lanes, the high mountain road and the coastal road, converged in Taif. Its regularly abundant supplies made the city an important staging post for the many caravans. Factors such as excellent agricultural land, pleasant climate, ample water, and convenience to the holy places (during both pre-Islamic and Islamic times), were responsible for Taif's long prosperity.

The name Taif comes from the Arabic word, meaning 'to surround'. The earliest settlers used to build protective walls around their crops. Eventually, defenses required a large wall around the entire expanded community which had spread over two square kilometres.

Taif's landscape is peppered with relics of its colourful past. Evidence of Turkish occupation appears in the form of garrisons and fortifications. Probably the oldest sign of early habitation can be found at a hillock of large rocks in an otherwise flat area of ground. Animal drawings and south Arabian script, the precursor of Arabic, can be seen on many of the rock faces. Experts date the carvings to 650 BC.

In the days of the trade routes, Taif served as a welcome refuge from the hardships of a long, arduous journey. In more recent times it has become a retreat from the oppressive summer heat of Jeddah and other lowland areas. Wealthy merchants built mansions and palaces in Taif, starting a trend which almost doubles the city's population to over 550,000 in peak periods.

The beautiful, forested mountain region of Al-Shafa ('the cure') has become a main place of relaxation. At 2,300 metres the visitor can witness breathtaking views of soaring peaks and verdant valleys. Prickly pears, a favourite fruit of tourists, grow here in profusion. The observant eye will also see wild lavender fighting for space between the rock crevices at the higher elevations. This continues to be an important ingredient in Taif's traditional perfume industry.

On the Taif-Makkah road rests the secondary mountain resort, 2,000 metre Al-Hada ('tranquility'). In order to preserve the natural beauty of Al-Shafa and Al-Hada, a Royal Decree forbids further construction in both areas.

The modern-day growth of Taif was due primarily to its designation as summer capital. Prior to the rule of King Fahad, the entire Saudi government used to uproot from Riyadh and establish itself in Taif during the hot summer months. During the Gulf War, Taif served as the seat of Kuwait's government in exile. Major support projects have helped to restore some of the city's former prosperity.

In history Taif has enjoyed a number of distinctions, not least of which is the fact that it minted the first Arab coins 1,300 years ago and that it introduced the first democratic government in the Arab world.

Despite the advances of time, Taif continues to distinguish itself as a place of beauty and a satisfying sanctuary from the pressures of the faster-paced world beyond its boundaries. *See also* PERFUME PRODUCTION.

TAMARISK. The flowering, greenish-blue tamarisks are common wherever there is adequate water. Locally crafted incense burners are frequently made with the easily available tamarisk wood. There are seven species of the genera *tamarix* in Saudi Arabia. The tree varieties (*athl*) can grow up to 15 metres tall. They are cultivated for their shade and as effective windbreaks. In coastal areas tamarisk help prevent soil erosion. The bushy shrubs (*tarfa*) range from a height of two to three metres for the *Tamarix mascatensis* found in northern Saudi Arabia to the widely distributed five metre tall *Tamarix nilotica. See also* FLORA.

TAQIYAH. A white skull cap (*taqiyah*) is worn by Saudi men under the *ghutra/shamagh*. The *taqiyah* helps to hold the head covering in place. *See also* BISHT; DRESS; FARWA; GHUTRAH; IGAAL; SIRWAAL.

TARHA. This black gauze hair covering is worm by Muslim women in public from the time they reach puberty. Islam requires women to cover their hair so that it does not cause temptation to men. *See also* ABAYA; BURQA; DRESS; WOMEN'S DRESS; VEIL.

TARUT ISLAND. This small island, now accessible from Qatif by a causeway, is the site of the oldest town yet discovered in Arabia. Once part of the Bahrain-based Dilmun culture, its strategic location made it an important military stronghold and a thriving commercial centre for trade between Arabia, Mesopotamia, Persia, and India.

The substantial and well preserved Tarut Fort sits atop a 16th century Portuguese fort and other ruins which are thought to date from 3000 BC. A permit from the Department of Antiquities is needed to visit the site. The picturesque island with its community of fishermen and weavers is a popular destination for photographers.

TEA. In formal circumstances, sweet tea is customarily served after the Arabic coffee and dates. Less formally, Saudis drink tea in copious quantities throughout the day. It is sipped from small, handled glasses that hold roughly triple the quantity of the coffee cups.

In addition to the commonly consumed fresh mint or black leaf tea, brews made from herbs, spices, and flowers are also popular. Not only are they refreshing beverages, they also may be used for medicinal purposes or, in the case of ginger tea, to provide quick warmth on cold winter nights.

TELEVISION. In a move to bring the modern world to Saudi Arabia, the late King Faisal introduced television to the country in the mid 1970s. In order to show concerned religious officials that television could have a positive impact, initial programming focused on readings from the *Qur'an*, religious discussions, and non-controversial presentations. King Faisal was later assassinated by a nephew, indirectly as a result of this progressive move.

Today, the programme content of the two English language and one Arabic language government-operated Saudi TV channels has expanded but the mandate remains conservative. To emphasise the adherence to Islamic principles, programming is interrupted for prayers. The many satellite TV channels now available have become popular alternatives to the local channels.

TENT. *See* BEDOUIN TENTS.

THOBE. Saudi men traditionally wear a full-length, long-sleeved, garment called a *thobe*. Buttons at the neck and give the *thobe* the appearance of a long shirt. The design includes deep pockets on the left and right sides. Most also have a breast pocket.

Materials vary, from fine cottons to inexpensive polyester. Islam prohibits Muslim men from wearing silk. Throughout the year, white *thobes* predominate but some men wear darker *thobes* made from worsted wool in winter. Colours may range from cream to grey to black or brown. For added warmth, a vest or Western-style suit jacket is worn with the *thobe*.

Thobes keep the wearer cool by a chimney effect which draws air in at the bottom and allows it to circulate effectively, unimpeded by tight-waisted apparel. *See also* BISHT; DRESS; FARWA; GHUTRAH; IGAAL; SIRWAAL; TAGIA.

TIHAMA. The word 'tihama' means 'a low place of high heat and calm winds'. The Saudi Arabian portion of this long, narrow lowland strip of land lies between the Red Sea and the Hijaz mountains that run from the southern Asir region all the way to Jeddah, a distance of 450 kilometres. With a maximum width of only 45 kilometres, the hot, dusty plains of the Tihama are home to tribes that were more influenced by African culture than Arabian. Centuries ago, Africans travelled north to Arabia as traders and pilgrims. The lifestyle, vivid dress, and even the vocabulary of the inhabitants of the Tihama reveal lingering evidence of this transfer of culture.

The distinctive, thatched, rondavel homes in the Tihama

A rondavel house, typical of the Tihama region.

T

are architectural reminders of the African heritage. Brightly coloured paintwork, so typical of the Asir, livens up the interiors of these simple reed and mud-plastered homes,

Tihama tribes have become renowned for their colourful and finely woven baskets, mats, hats, and containers. The people also earn incomes from fishing and traditional agriculture. Farmers irrigate the otherwise arid land by diverting mountain run-offs.

In certain places on the Tihama coastal plains one can witness the black, hardened lava of ancient volcanic activity. This zone supports small shrubs, annuals, and such unusual vegetation as the chunky elephant tree which stores water and combats erosion through its extensive root system. *See also* ARCHITECTURE; ASIR.

TOLA. The tola is a traditional weight equivalent to approximately one ounce or 30 grams. Gold of this weight is pressed into bars for convenience. Although still available, gold tola bars are fast being replaced by less charming plastic credit cards.

TOMB. *See* MADAIN SALEH

TRADE ROUTE. *See* FRANKINCENSE ROUTE.

TRAIN. *See* RAILWAY.

TRIBE. In order to minimise vulnerability to raids, small, independent households banded together for protection. Although tribal associations began with the bedouin, settled urban and rural groups also have a tribal identity.

A tribe in Saudi Arabia is a large family grouping descended from a common paternal ancestor and headed by a male leader called a *shaikh*. The tribe may be subdivided by up to six of these patrilineal lineages. A tribe consists of families (the smallest grouping) and clans. A tribe may have as few as 50 members and as many as several hundred. Saudis identify themselves culturally and socially by their tribes.

Loyalty to the family is paramount, followed by loyalty to the tribe and, in distant third place, to the state. Honour or dishonour on an individual is assumed by the tribe. For example, if one member is wronged, vengeance is the responsibility of the entire lineage. The tribe also offers support to its members in time of need, a precursor to the welfare state. Although each tribe values its independence, individual members are expected to conform to group mores.

Tribal territories, with their vital grazing grounds and water sources, were vigorously defended. Before centralized government, the entire peninsula fell under the jurisdiction of various tribal leaders. Each *shaikh* made himself available to his tribesmen through a system of open audience called a *majlis*. At such gatherings, any subject could present his grievance or make his opinions known. It was the duty of the *shaikh* to dispense justice, food, or clothing as fairly as possible. Although their autonomy has been eroded, tribal leaders/*shaikhs* still enjoy enormous respect and remain influential decision makers.

Political changes and the rapid advances of technology have inevitably influenced certain aspects of tribal life. Neverthless, valuable loyalties and support prevail, features which have proved useful as a network system for employment or assistance. *See also* BEDOUIN; SHAIKH.

U

ULAMA. These religious leaders include scholars, judges, lawyers, religious teachers, and *imams*. The king consults regularly with the Council of Senior Ulama. The tacit approval of the *ulama* enables the government to introduce potentially controversial policies. The government, on the other hand, gives legitimacy to the religious body.

ULULATION. Saudi women make this shrill sound, called *zaghareet* in Arabic, with a rapid vibration of the tongue against the back of the upper teeth while holding a high-pitched note. To increase the ululation, the woman might tap four fingers of the right hand on the mouth. Women ululate to express emotion such as joy at weddings or sadness at death.

UMRAH. Pilgrimage to Makkah is one of the five pillars of Islam. The *hajj*, performed at a specific time of the year, should be performed once in each Muslim's lifetime.

Umrah is similar to *hajj* except it is an individual act of pilgrimage performed at other times during the year. Although not equivalent to the *hajj*, it nevertheless is a source of great blessings, particularly if performed during Ramadan. The Prophet Muhammad said, *To perform umrah in Ramadan is like performing the hajj with me.*

UNAYZEH. Formerly the principal city of Qassim, Unayzeh still retains the charm of a lost age, although many of its old buildings have disappeared. The Wadi Rima separates Unayzeh from its neighbour Buraydah which has now surpassed Unayzeh in importance.

The people of Unayzeh have always enjoyed a reputation for generous hospitality. Philby remarked, *It seemed to me that I had stepped suddenly...into a highly civilised, even cultured society...in this gem among Arabian cities....*

V

VEIL. Although it is not an obligation of Islam (in fact the religion requires faces to be uncovered during prayer), Saudi tradition demands that women and girls from the age of puberty cover their faces.

Veils consist of a fine black gauze or chiffon that completely covers the face. Some tie behind the head, others sit on the hair and fall over the face. Depending on the style of the veil, there can be slits for the eyes or the fabric can be solid. In some parts of the country, the veils may be decorated with embroidery, beads, or coins.

Before modern circumstances began to erode old traditions, young girls eagerly anticipated the time when they could wear the veil, a sign of their maturity. The veil allows a woman to remain modest while at the same time to be flirtatiously revealing. Depending on the design of the veil, it often accentuates a woman's beauty, if not in reality then certainly in the imagination of the beholder. *See also* ABAYA; BURQA; DRESS; TARHA; WOMEN'S DRESS.

W

WADI. A *wadi* is the Arabic word meaning riverbed. Throughout most of the year, these are merely dry depressions of varying widths and depths that cut across the land. During heavy rains, they fill quickly and carry the water in rapid torrents along an ancient route. In periods of sustained rainfall the *wadis* may remain as rivers for some time, serving as a magnet to all life forms.

WAHHABISM. This movement's 18th century founder, Muhammad ibn Abdul-Wahhab, believed that decadence had crept into the practice of Islam. He advocated a return to its purist origins. After several unsuccessful attempts at moral reform, Abdul-Wahhab met Muhammad Al-Saud, the ruler of the desert oasis of Dir'iyyah. They formed an alliance based on their common religious ideology: Al-Saud vowed he and his family would always rule according to the tenets of Islam; Abdul-Wahhab promised he and his followers would support the Al-Sauds politically. Neither leader could anticipate the impact of this bond which became instrumental not only in an Islamic revival on the peninsula but, eventually, in the secular authority and domination of the Al-Sauds throughout much of Arabia.

Abdul-Wahhab became known by the honorific title of Al-Sheikh. His family was referred to as Al Al-Sheikh. They remain influential in religious and government matters and are one of the families with whom the Al-Saud intermarry.

Although popularly referred to in English as 'Wahhabis', the correct term for the followers of the religious reformer is *Muwahhidun*, meaning 'unitarians'. *See also* ISLAM.

WATCH TOWER. Strategically placed watch towers (*qasba*) are a hallmark of the southwest region of Saudi Arabia. They stretch in an unbroken series along the route from Taif to the Asir. The literal translation of the Arabic is 'sticks', an appropriate description since they look like sticks standing on the hillsides.

Qasbas were constructed with stone or mud, depending on the material which prevailed in the area. As a precaution against erosion by heavy rains, mud *qasbas* had layers of slate inserted horizontally into the outer walls.

The larger towers are a legacy from Turkish invaders. Smaller *qasbas* served either as communication posts between tribes, as guard stations for the protection of each village's fields and herds, or for the storage of grain.

Nowadays, these abandoned towers serve the more romantic purpose of making the spectacular scenery come alive with a sense of history and of allowing modern travellers to let their own imaginings take them where they haven't been.

WEAVING. *See* BEDOUIN WEAVING.

WEDDING. *See* MARRIAGE.

WEDDING PALACE. In previous generations, wedding celebrations took place in homes and private gardens. When luxury hotels became more prevalent in the Kingdom, it became the fashion to hire the function rooms. Now the most common venue is a wedding palace, a purpose-built hall that can accommodate large numbers of guests.

The interiors of wedding palaces are often ornately fitted. The main room consists of numerous rows of theatre-style seating facing a central aisle which leads to a stage where the bride and groom sit. Female musicians playing traditional instruments sit to the side of the stage.

A separate room for buffet-style dining is adjacent to the main hall. Although most of the food is catered, some families also provide traditional home-cooked dishes.

Due to space constraints of homes and hotels, men's and women's parties usually were held in different locations. Wedding palaces make it possible for both groups to celebrate in one place while still remaining separate.

WIND TOWER. In the days before electric cooling systems, Saudis used the ingenious construction of wind towers (*badjeer*) to give them respite from the heat.

The wood- or stone-built structures usually rise one or two storeys above the building they are cooling. This height allows them to trap breezes, even when there is no wind. The towers may be built as part of the building or constructed adjacent to the structure and connected by a tunnel. Air enters through the four-sided openings at the top of

the tower and is channelled down the shaft, providing ventilation to the lower level. These openings can be closed in the cooler months or during sand storms.

WOMEN'S DRESS. The traditional, regional Saudi dresses are full-length, long-sleeved, loose-fitting shifts, usually with a round neck. The normally black fabric has front panels that are intricately embroidered in colourful geometric patterns. Dresses for special occasions might be decorated with sequins, coins, shells, or metallic thread.

Nowadays, most Saudi women wear long, loose dresses or Western-style clothes under their abayas and in the privacy of their homes. Western-style bridal gowns have also become a popular alternative to the traditional dresses. *See also* ABAYA; BURQA; SHAYLA; TARHA; VEIL.

Y

YANBU. In former times, Yanbu benefited from its location on a major caravan route. Its closeness to Makkah and Madinah made it a safe and convenient resting point for a regular influx of pilgrims and assured it of commercial prosperity. As ships and planes became the preferred conveyance for pilgrims, however, the town was reduced to a sleepy fishing village.

Saudi Arabia's oil boom brought renewed importance to Yanbu. Because of its proximity to the Suez Canal and European markets, Yanbu was chosen in the 1970s as one of two sites for major oil-related industrialization. Together with Jubail on the Kingdom's east coast, the villages were completely transformed.

The building of a physical infrastructure included ports, airports, more than 560 kilometres of roads, and utilities at the two sites. Extensive harbour facilities and easy access to international airports have contributed to Jubail's and Yanbu's status as powerful industrial cities.

Vital water supplies are provided by desalination plants which can produce up to 56,000 cubic metres for Yanbu.

Z

ZAKAT. *See* ISLAM.

ZATAR. In the Middle East, this aromatic mixture of sesame seeds, sumac, and thyme is most frequently used as a topping on pita bread. The blend can also be added to minced beef or vegetables or used as an ingredient in dips. zatar is high in phosphates and is said to increase memory. See SPICES.

ZAMZAM WATER. In a test imposed by God, Abraham (Ibrahim) was instructed to lead his wife Hagar and their infant son Ishmael (Ismail) into the arid valley of Makkah and trust them to God's care. Hagar soon became frantic for the survival of her child. Leaving Ishmael in a safe place, she ran seven times between the mountains of Al-Safa and Marwa in an unsuccessful search for water. Finally, Hagar climbed to the top of each mountain, imploring God's help. The sounds of animals brought renewed fear for Ishmael's safety. When she returned to him, she found the baby drinking and playing with water that was miraculously seeping from the ground beneath his cheek.

Hagar granted the guardianship of the water source that was named Zamzam to the Jarham tribe who made the area a place of settlement. When Abraham returned to Makkah, he dug the well deeper and, commanded by God, built the holy *ka'ba* nearby. Makkah has been a site of pilgrimage ever since.

For many generations, the well remained under the protection of the Jarham tribe. Although there are conflicting stories, for whatever reason, Zamzam was then concealed for several centuries. The location was eventually revealed to Abdul Muttalib, the grandfather of the Prophet Muhammad, in a dream. He succeeded in unearthing the miraculous well and remained its guardian.

Since that time, the abundant waters of Zamzam have never ceased to flow. The facilities were modernised in 1945 and 1976. Now, an elaborate system of pipes and filters brings specially cooled water to the faithful via hundreds of faucets.

According to tradition, whoever drinks the sacred waters of Zamzam will have his wishes granted. It has therefore become customary to make a supplication (Allah, I pray for wisdom, good fortune, and good health) followed by a more personal request to respond to immediate needs. Zamzam water is also said to cure skin and eye infections and to relieve stomach cramps.

ZUBAYDAH ROAD. Overland pilgrim and caravan routes, although well travelled, always subjected the travellers to risks and hardships. Crossing wide stretches of deserts was particularly hazardous.

In the ninth century, Zubaydah, the cousin and favourite wife of Harun Al-Rashid, the Abbasid Caliph of Baghdad, nearly died from thirst on her pilgrimage to Makkah. As a devout and caring Muslim, she vowed not to let other pilgrims suffer a similar misfortune.

In order to ease the journey, she organised the

construction of palaces and public rest houses (*caravansarai*) and, more importantly, hundreds of wells and cisterns along the route between Kufa (now in southern Iraq) and Makkah. These were built at intervals of no more than 40 kilometres. Some of the larger cisterns could provide water for more than 5,000 pilgrims. Where the route traversed sandy desert, large sections of flagstones were laid. Milestones posted at each station informed travellers of the distance between Kufa and Makkah.

The 1,300-kilometre road became known as the *Darb Zubaydah*, or Zubaydah Road. Even after 1,200 years, some of the watering points still function. Today, they are mostly used by bedouin to water their animals.

Acknowledgements

The information contained in these pages has come from many sources. Much of it has been gathered over the 25 years in the Kingdom; some of it has been acquired or expanded upon recently, specifically for this book.

To everyone who has added to my better understanding of Saudi Arabia, thank you.

In particular, I would like to thank Lillie Arnaout, Nic Coombs, Sean Cuddihy, Tara Cuddihy, Mary Daley, Ingrid Galal, and Mayssam Tamim who have been so generous with their time and expertise in helping me compile the information for this book.

KC September 2001

OTHER BOOKS BY KATHY CUDDIHY:

Motherhood: Marriage's Occupational Hazard
Familiarity Breeds Content
Saudi Customs and Etiquette
The Hostess Book
Gifts of Arabia